Pagan Portals

Maman Brigitte

Dark Goddess of Africa and Ireland

Pagan Portals

Maman Brigitte

Dark Goddess of Africa and Ireland

Pauline Breen

MOON
BOOKS

London, UK
Washington, DC, USA

CollectiveInk

First published by Moon Books, 2024
Moon Books is an imprint of Collective Ink Ltd.,
Unit 11, Shepperton House, 89 Shepperton Road, London, N1 3DF
office@collectiveinkbooks.com
www.collectiveinkbooks.com
www.moon-books.net

For distributor details and how to order please visit the 'Ordering' section on our website.

Text copyright: Pauline Breen 2023

ISBN: 978 1 80341 736 3
978 1 80341 735 6 (ebook)
Library of Congress Control Number: 2023950989

A CIP catalogue record for this book is available from the British Library.

Design: Lapiz Digital Services

UK: Printed and bound by CPI Group (UK) Ltd, Croydon, CR0 4YY
Printed in North America by CPI GPS partners

We operate a distinctive and ethical publishing philosophy in all areas of our business, from our global network of authors to production and worldwide distribution.

Contents

Introduction   1

Chapter 1 Maman Brigitte in Haiti   17
    Her Name Variations   17
    Vodou in Haiti   17
    History of Haiti   18
    Yoruba   20
    Haitian Vodou Principles   23
    The Lwa in Haitian Vodou   25
    The Gede Lwa   27
    Maman Brigitte in Haitian Vodou   28

Chapter 2 Maman Brigitte in Louisiana   42
    Voodoo in New Orleans   42
    History of New Orleans   45
    The Irish in New Orleans   47
    Irish Women in New Orleans   50
    Irish Women and Haitian Women's Common
        Experience in New Orleans   58
    Maman Brigitte in New Orleans   60

Chapter 3 Maman Brigitte in Today's World   66
    Maman Brigitte   66
    Colours Associated with Maman Brigitte   74
    Animals Associated with Maman Brigitte   76
    Symbols Associated with Maman Brigitte   77
    Days Associated with Maman Brigitte   78
    Offerings to Maman Brigitte   79
    Connecting to Maman Brigitte   79

Conclusion   82
Bibliography   86

For Brigid

Introduction

Can Brigid of Ireland be considered a dark goddess? I think so. The Great African Mother, from whom all life came, subdivided and re-embodied all over the globe. The Goddess Brigid was her Irish and Celtic expression. As the birthing mother, she continues to rebirth and reinvent herself for the needs of her people in different times. In one part of the world, she is named Athena, in another Shakti and in yet another, Rhiannon. In Ireland, one name for her is Brigid. Brigid as the Great Mother reincarnation also continues to rebirth and reinvent herself for the needs of her people. Whatever they need she gives them, wherever they go, she goes, whomever they need, she is.

Maman Brigitte came into being on a small island known once as Ayiti and now as Haiti. She was born into a religion known as Vodou from the wails of despair, terror and anguish within the shackles of slavery. Her people, now enslaved, had been brought over from the Yoruba region in Africa where Oya, the great goddess of the river Nile was a key deity. In a new land, far away from Africa, Maman Brigitte would be birthed from a fusion of the Goddess Oya and Brigid, Goddess and Saint of Ireland. What was Brigid doing in Haiti or Africa I hear you ask. We will explore this in a later chapter. But in short, as part of indentured servitude and as part of trade with Benin in West Africa, the Irish and the Breton Celts (Brittany as a Celtic country also worshipped Brigid) were found in this part of the world.

Maman Brigitte emerged as a result of slavery. She embodied rage, grief and terror as a voice for her enslaved persons but also became a symbol of comfort in the form of a wise and loving mother who not only bore witness to the suffering of her children but became an iconic symbol of strength and hope. As a figure in Haitian Vodou she would play her role within the religious construct of Vodou that brought French colonialism in Haiti to its knees and push Haiti into the spotlight as the first black republic, ever, to gain Independence. Brigitte assisted in liberating her people. In the aftermath, Haitians would take Brigitte with them as they set sail for a nearby overseas department of France to make a fresh start following the overthrow of France. Their new home would be in the Deep South in New Orleans, Louisiana. With Brigitte guiding them to a new land, Haitians would merge with Irish immigrants who had already made New Orleans their home and who arrived in significant numbers during and after the famine in Ireland. As a result, Maman Brigitte evolved into a powerful dark goddess as a consequence of increasing exposure to the Irish immigrant community who were predominantly Catholic and who had a reverence for Saint Brigid. It is said that the practice of Vodou reached a peak in popularity in Louisiana during the antebellum period where many Haitian and Irish immigrants were co-living as new citizens of New Orleans. It is my belief that the somewhat shared common experience of both Haitians and Irish in the New World, particularly the shared experience of Haitian and Irish women, propelled Maman Brigitte forward as a strong mother figure and key deity in their newfound home.

Out of murky, swampy waters in the Mississippi, New Orleans rose as a unique entity who witnessed and understood hardship that came with upheaval and displacement and who also represented strength and stamina to root down and grow in new soil. She came to represent survival and the coming togetherness of all vulnerable people beginning new lives in the New World. As Haitians and the Irish found their homes in tenements or in wealthy homes as domestics, Brigitte was found, along with her partner Baron Samedi in the cemetery. The cemetery is her home. Here, in tranquillity, she flits between both worlds of the living and the dead similar also to

2

the Goddess Brigid who transcended the Otherworld and the living world.

In comparison to Brigid who is most typically associated with the light and the coming of Spring, Brigitte is a goddess of death. She is the lady of the night. Within the dark, Brigitte is revered for reclaiming all those who lived on the fringes of society in life and gather them into her family in death as they wander aimlessly in the spirit world. In death she gives them a place of belonging, that they may never would have experienced in life. This is what possibly made her known as a great mother figure. A mother in the living world and also beyond the veil of death. Brigitte was also worshipped as protectress of their graves in the living world, warding off zombies returning from beyond the veil. From the quiet cemetery she notices all evil actions in life and call them out in death, and so, is a symbol for justice, especially for women and children. This role as justice keeper was also associated with Brigid of Ireland. Maman Brigitte evolved into a figure that was much loved but also feared. With her large eyes there is nothing that she could not see in the light and in the dark. Her skin is deathly pale which is another reason why she is often compared to Brigid of Ireland. But in personality she is quite different to Brigid.

Brigitte in contrast to Brigid is sensual, sexual and is associated with a most provocative dance known as the Banda, to arouse sexual feelings. Sex is the ultimate expression of life. If Brigitte emerged during hardship, she definitely reminds her devotees of the importance of taking pleasure in life anywhere they can. Life is short. She is known to enjoy a cigar or cigarettes and take a glass or two of rum. This aspect of her made her accessible to her peoples. She knew how to have a good time without materialism and would demonstrate the joy that can also be found in life amongst the most atrocious conditions. Her followers understood her ability to enter all worlds easily, which made her immortal and who could transcend time. As the lady of the night and associated with the dark realm, Brigitte became synonymous with all issues pertaining to the dark, most notably death, as well as deep, shadow work. In the depths of darkness, she emits her fiery light and is through her light a silent presence not only for grief, loss and lament but also a symbol of hope for easier times to come.

For those brave to enter their individual darkness and pain she became the epitome of backbone, a formidable *femme* to showcase human strength especially strong women. Herself, born out of enforced slavery and flourishing in a muddy swamp, who better than her to showcase survival? Brigitte showcased death as a significant physical transformation that is inevitable for us all. She would remind us to take pleasure in life but to be accountable for all our actions in death. This would not only input a serious undertone into the melody of life but also assure those victimised by injustice in this world that their day of justice would come. As guardian of the cemetery and fluid traveller between all worlds, she would assure us of her unspeaking, motherly presence when our time comes to depart the living world. She, the dark goddess of the cemetery, is the enigmatic and obscure Maman Brigitte.

I officially dedicated as Priestess of Brigid in January 2023. In the lead up to my dedication, particularly around Samhain (October 31st) I became more and more intrigued by the darkness and the concept of the dark goddess. I was drawn to the colour black, to black crystals and to looking at my own dark shadow parts in need of recognition never mind healing. I would never really consider myself a lover of the dark as I generally struggle with winter and the absence of light, so it didn't really feel like 'me' but 'me', whoever that is, continues to grow and develop or to put it another way, continues to journey deeper into a more profound layer of authenticity that seems more possible with advancing age. I didn't dismiss my newfound interest in the dark as I knew it had most definitely come from encountering Maman Brigitte whilst researching Brigid.

When researching my book *This is Brigid – Goddess & Saint of Ireland* I came across a mention of Brigid as Maman Brigitte in Haitian Vodou. I was utterly enthralled by the fact that she is a Haitian/Louisianan Lwa/Loa (spirit) of death. This seemed the very antithesis as to what she represented as the bringer of new life here in Ireland. I was dying to find out (pardon the pun) why she was so linked to death in this culture and why she was sometimes painted with her mouth sealed as though she were voiceless. This too, contrasted with her symbolism in Ireland as queen of oration, goddess of poetry and life giver by her sacred breath. In fact, as goddess she represents all things linked to communication, so seeing her often depicted as mute was intriguing.

Stumbling across Maman Brigitte was like a furnace door opened and a burst of fire rushed out that screamed 'here I am, here I am'. Reluctantly, I had to close that door to maintain focus. I had to concentrate and not allow myself to go down a rabbit hole like I usually would. But in closing the furnace door, I acknowledged I had felt a different energy with the mere pronunciation of Maman Brigitte and once the time was right, I would give it the respect and time needed to explore her in this aspect.

Once my first book was completed, I felt her familiar prod to get cracking and honour my promise. This is where I can testify that Brigid is anything but soft and gentle which are words often used to describe her. She is insistent when a) she wants something, b) you've promised her something and c) she knows you'll love it (which I did). When all three of these line up you can rest assured there will be a significant push to start. When the time was right, I started to dream about areas I would need to research for Maman Brigitte. Often, these would wake me up in the early hours of the morning with thoughts and ideas racing through my mind. I would need to enter the world of Vodou as it is spelled in Haitian culture and understand what circumstances in Haitian and Louisianan history not only birthed Maman Brigitte but allowed her to flourish. This felt out of my comfort zone and intellectual depth. And I doubted if I had the right to write about a culture with which I have no direct contact. However, in my down time, my mind started to piece together earlier parts of my own life that were significant to researching Brigid as the Vodun/Voodoo deity Maman Brigitte.

In my twenties I travelled to an oversees department of France called La Réunion where I spent a year as an Erasmus student. This is now a long time ago and how I wish I had been there with the same open eyes as I now have to the Réunionnais cultural and religious practices. There is only so much a twenty-year-old can understand, especially one that has been submerged in Catholicism. I don't remember very much of that time, but I do remember standing and watching a man in his garden practising Voodoo. His house and garden were at the bottom of the road where I was living. Of course, I didn't understand what he was doing, and it scared me, but it also really fascinated me. On this island I studied French and had a particular interest in African feminine literature which I absorbed as part of my course. Looking back now, it seems as though Brigid had always been around me with me growing up in Ireland but even as far as the Indian ocean she was there, entwined and embedded in local Vodou practices as Maman Brigitte.

I consider Brigid a multi-faceted Goddess that continues to twirl and reveal different aspects of herself. Maman Brigitte is one such aspect. This makes Brigid such a unique deity. Apart from the fact that she is the only pagan deity to have been swept into Christianity, leaving that aside for a while, it just fascinates me how she continues to rebirth, blend and become whatever is needed by people. The needs of her devotees is what defines Brigid. She is the definition of fluid and modern and this is what makes her accessible to everybody, of any creed, gender, culture. She is never static, and I love her for this. For me, she represents life flow and life is constantly in flux. I see her as the ultimate Mother Goddess who becomes and appears as to what her children need, wherever they are and no matter what dire situations they find themselves in. Throughout this book I will endeavour to express this through a variety of language that will hopefully make sense. I will refer to Maman Brigitte as an expression/version/aspect/appearance/persona of Brigid that hopefully will help paint a picture of how I sense her. One thing that continues to become clear to me whilst working with the divine feminine is that nothing is ever compartmentalised, black or white, or nothing connected to her can ever be easily defined. The Goddess, by her very essence is a mystery. She is chaos that begins with the beginning of life found in blood and mucus at birth. She gives us life and watches over us as autonomous beings without defining or limiting our behaviours. This is in stark contrast to most patriarchal religions that demand certain life choices in order to belong. The Goddess is free and ever evolving. I find this so comforting because I understand that no matter how life develops during my time here on earth, this energy of the divine feminine will reveal herself into a specific aspect to help us that is unique to our needs of our times. Maman Brigitte is, of course, not unique to our times, but she is in my opinion, underused as a dark goddess figure as we all navigate through issues today that were also pertinent during the time of her emergence. Issues such as war, displacement, homelessness, injustice, misogyny and issues relating to our personal shadows which is our responsibility to face.

By connecting to Brigid, I reconnected to a feminine, energetic universal life force within me that has been intentionally removed from the world at the hands of patriarchy. I reconnected to the sacred feminine, the Great Mother, the divine feminine, the mama, the creatrix. Finally waking up and remembering her has helped me to feel like I have a footing here in this world as I, as a woman, have a role model that has my back and she's just fabulous. I remembered the sacred feminine through Brigid. Once I had remembered her, I needed to really discover or to begin my journey to my authentic self. And this is when Maman Brigitte raised her head significantly to call me to this journey. It was time. It would mean stripping away all that I had internalised from the patriarchy and moulded by familial and societal conditioning and discard it as I delved deep into the depths of my soul. It was the next obvious layer of working with the sacred feminine. Again, this brings me back to the chaos associated with the goddess. Unlike working with structured patriarchal religions, remembering our spiritual connection doesn't end with simply remembering. We don't remember or find our way back just to have an 'A ha' moment and leave it there. Once we remember our soulful origin, we need to get dirty and dig deep into the many layers of conditioning that we have had placed around us in order to resurrect or rebirth our true selves and be as close to our true selves as we can be.

To consciously begin my journey to authenticity I needed a unique energy that had come forward into the lives of people who had been literally stripped away of all material possessions and who were finding themselves walking on completely new soil. Everything outside of themselves that they had identified with was now gone. Brigitte was a symbol of this complete erosion down to the most basic essence within us, the soul. I needed strength through my personal tower moment. I needed someone to *ok* the death of things and to assure me that the new could only come in through the releasing of the old. The void after the removal of the old would be the portal for the new. Who was more suited to this than Maman Brigitte? And the best thing was, I didn't even need to move beyond Brigid for this. I just needed to go deeper down into her sacred energy and look at her from a different angle. And there she was. The Goddess Brigid, turning and twirling in slow motion, like a ballerina figurine, to enable me to see another aspect of her that had a similar but different name. Brigitte would show me a specific skillset that she possessed and that I could also discover in myself if I opened myself up to her.

And yet at that time I was unconsciously, already in her deathly realm of the graveyard. I was mourning and lamenting pieces of myself that were no more. On a physical level, this was an ever-changing menopausal body in which I felt no familiarity. On an emotional level I needed to let a part of me die but I was struggling with the releasing of the familiar for the unknown. Thankfully, my connection to the Goddess would help me navigate through my darkness. And through this darkness her appearance and energy felt different as I leaned into those heavy feelings. A sombre, silent presence was now witnessing my inner struggles, and this felt very different to the vibe that I feel with the Goddess Brigid. So silent was Brigitte, I felt like I was losing my connection to Brigid. She seemed far away, and this frustration added to the hopelessness. I was having a different experience and what I was experiencing was in fact, a descent into my darkness. And in this darkness Brigid turned her other cheek that gave her a different identity as Brigitte. It was up to me then to cultivate a personal relationship with this aspect of her so that I could feel this energy and tap into it. In working with Brigitte, I came to feel and understand how we are all composed of the light and dark. If we ignore the dark part of ourselves, we can only lead a semi-fulfilling and half-life because we are denying half of who we are or only telling half of our story. Because Maman Brigitte deals with deeply repressed issues, this is why I sense her as a dark goddess.

We call the Dark Goddess the Goddess of the Underworld, Goddess of Death. She rules over everything we fear and every aspect of ourselves where we feel shame. While it is true that one Goddess may have more pronounced darker qualities than another, we need to see both the light *and* dark qualities within each and every Goddess archetype. This is crucial, I think, if we are to be honest about our own light and dark qualities and if we are to use the Goddess as a sacred roadmap for our lives. The notion of perfectionism inherent in our society, especially for women is built solely on the light qualities that are considered acceptable. We live in a toxic 'love and light' society that is unbalanced and unattainable *all* the time.

The darker aspects of the divine feminine are awaiting recognition and reverence on a collective level. These aspects within the divine, like in women, are ignored, frowned upon or buried into disappearance. A fine example would be the madness attached to the rage of Kali-Ma. If these aspects of the divine feminine continue to be vilified then our source of connection and guidance through these deities is not as powerful as it could be and we continue to struggle in an inauthentic world that refuses to wholly accept us women, for all that we are.

Why is society so afraid of these dark goddesses? Strong powerful goddesses such as the Morrigan, Kali-Ma, Hekate, Sekhmet and Maman Brigitte. Why have they been so vilified for us, especially us, as women? Why is rage shunned as a means of screaming STOP? Why are death and our ancestors not regularly discussed even though our towns and villages contain all of our deceased loved ones within cemeteries. The dead world touches our living world and vice versa but we endeavour to keep them separate as them and us. These dark goddesses can help us understand the cycle of life that involves death and help us feel part of the natural rhythm of the world if we acknowledge them.

Brigid is a Goddess of extreme depth and contains both the light and the dark. On the surface she is the Goddess of Spring, of Fire as well as healing, poetry and smithcraft. We tend to look at these three aspects as positive and, of course, there is also a darker side to these. Fire can destroy as well as function positively for warmth or illumination. Words in poetry can ridicule or call something or someone out and smithcraft is, in its very essence, the death of one thing in order for something else to be constructed.

Even in Irish mythology and lore surrounding Brigid I feel so much darkness with her. A darkness that is deep beneath the earth as Mother Goddess, all the way through bones and minerals down in her womb. This place where we return home in death known as the Otherworld. The Otherworld was sacred to our Celtic Irish ancestors. It was a place where all earthly suffering ended and life in a different form continued. Brigid is deeply connected to the Otherworld, not only as shapeshifter between worlds but also as daughter of the God of the Otherworld, An Dagda.

This darkness that I experience with Brigid is solid and tenacious. There's no breaking her strong hold. She's got your back. There is no time in our lives where we feel as vulnerable as when we experience death and there is nothing darker than death itself. Yet we rarely associate Brigid with death. But Brigid was the original keener of Ireland. As keener she gave voice to grief and honoured the pain experienced with loss. With resolution, she held the grief and through keening, managed to release it healthily and purposefully. Also, in ancient Irish practice, she was the strong psychopomp of the recently departed, who brought souls to their eternal home. Brigid was the resilient energy that Irish people beseeched in their dark moments of witnessing and experiencing death. But this changed. Death became something we feared. We stopped seeing time as cyclical where death and life went hand in hand, and we started to see it as linear with death being the final stop. The dark came to be viewed as diabolic, evil, something to be feared. We started to extend vast amounts of energy in fighting the appearance of advancing age and approaching death which has resulted in a society obsessed with keeping young and valuing youth. Over time, our natural acceptance of death evolved into a strained relationship for us all. We ignored it until it inevitably arrived at our doorstep and then we adopted the stiff upper lip approach to our grief rather than expressing our loss. We turned our backs on our communities for support, put on a brave face and returned to normal duties at the speed of light as though nothing had happened. This has had a huge knock-on effect as to how we view life and our own existence. With us not acknowledging death as a natural part of our lives we view our prestigious places in our family lineages with apathy and stop venerating our ancestors who played an important role in getting us to this point where we are now experiencing life. Ancestral acknowledgement and veneration had been a huge part of early Celtic life. Samhain was the season with the arrival of the darkness where ancestors were particularly remembered. Samhain/Fet Gede is also a significant time of year for Maman Brigitte.

With the focus constantly on the returning light and a new dawn, Brigid became most associated with these aspects and her hitherto role as death bringer and psychopump became overshadowed. The new wave of 'love and light' that we have integrated has come out of that. Love and light cannot prevail *all* the time. There is a season for Death and there is a season for Life. Each is a component of our lives and needs to be acknowledged. This doesn't always need to be connected to physical death. In our lives we regularly let something, or some situations die, such as a relationship, a job or a place of residence. This process of letting something die or letting something go is made harder by not acknowledging the impeccable timing for its arrival in our lives and the growth that has occurred so that death can show up as a timely signal for rebirth.

I think our unhealthy attitude to death has been due to the fact that, as a collective we have lost reverence for the Great Mother Goddess, the Sacred Feminine. We have lost our understanding of the process of life and the reason for life. Where Goddess centred religions and practices maintained their respect and worship for the Great Mother, death remained a respected inevitable part of life and as such strong ancestral veneration remained as a daily practice in the everyday lives of people. But not every culture allowed this to happen. For Haitians and Louisianans, Maman Brigitte is a deity very much linked to ancestral veneration, death and the deathly realm.

If there is one thing, that I have learned from working with Brigid is that the old always form part of the new and this is the viewpoint I very much hold with her. I see her first and foremost as Goddess who morphed into saint. How could I think that is where the mystery ends? That she is either A or B? Goddess or Saint. There is so much more to this beautiful spirit that never ceases to amaze me. I have always understood and felt that remembering and rediscovering the sacred feminine is actually a remembering and rediscovering of myself as a woman. As I explore her in various sub-divisions, I realise I explore myself. In exploring myself, I discover my shadows, but I feel I have the strength to begin healing these, through her. I also believe the darker aspects of the feminine represent the mother wound. The mother wound exists in many families and collectively. On a collective level, the Great Goddess as a whole has been repressed and replaced throughout history. But she is rising. As she rises, she demands total acceptance of her lightness *and* her darkness, of warts and all! She has a voice that needs to be heard. She has anger that needs to be expressed. She has power that needs space to be effective, aka, step aside Patriarchy, you've had your millennia, never mind your moment!

I knew I would be led on a powerful transformative journey working with Maman Brigitte. And this certainly lived up to my expectations. On a soul level I journeyed through a deeper level of acknowledgement and I encountered a powerful aspect of her that I can call upon to help me deal with the heavy stuff. On a physical level I journeyed to New Orleans in the Deep South to feel her spirit there. The Deep South has always fascinated me and now I had the best reason to go and experience her on her own turf. I couldn't wait to begin researching the unique persona of Maman Brigitte and opening myself totally to how I would feel this spirit and in turn work with this aspect of her. I wanted to see how this energy would be specific and how I could incorporate her into my own spiritual practice.

Who is Maman Brigitte? What does she stand for? And how can I work with her differently from the most familiar Brigid to me? These are the questions I will endeavour to answer. Before I delve into the content, I wish to make myself very clear when I say that I have no direct experience with either Haitian Vodou/Vodún or Louisianan Vodoo and I do not encourage random invocation of Vodou Lwa without specific training, understanding or guidance. Voodoo has never featured in my culture. I am no expert, nor do I claim to be. I am Irish and I am a Priestess of Brigid. I have a basis of Brigid to begin my exploration of her in various forms. The reason I pen this book is because it is my heart's desire to explore Brigid in ALL Her forms and the dark Goddess Maman Brigitte is one such aspect that very much caught my attention. By writing this book I want to share my experience and my research and show how the famous Green Mantle spread out, not only across the Curragh plains in Kildare, Ireland but in this specific exploration of Maman Brigitte to the Caribbean and the Americas.

Researching Brigid and sharing my findings makes my soul sing like the little linnet in the early morning. I know I am here to raise the collective awareness about the Goddess and my

Goddess is called Brigid. It is with that being said that I can proceed with my findings to share with you what I have learned. It is up to you to accept this alternative essence of Brigid or not. (It is only an alternative version of her in the western world.) I mean no cultural misappropriation and I recognise my colour of privilege entering the world of Maman Brigitte. But she has called for this, and her call is the one I listen to over any other.

Maman Brigitte – Dark Goddess of Africa and Ireland is divided into three chapters. In Chapter 1 I explore the history of Haiti, the specific Yoruba religious tradition that was brought from Africa to Haiti during the slave trade and Maman Brigitte in Haiti. It is important to me that I present the historical and religious backdrop before presenting Brigitte as both are paramount to understanding her and what she represents. In Chapter 2 I explore the history of New Orleans and how Haitian Vodou and Irish Catholicism melded and peaked in New Orleans as a result of mass immigration. I look at the specific contribution from Irish women and Haitian women to their new society in New Orleans and how this in turn impacted the evolvement of Maman Brigitte in Louisiana and who she is in the Deep South. In Chapter 3 I share my personal findings on colours, animals, days, symbols, and offerings connected to her and ways of working with her for your own practice or as something to build on or simply for information. I hope you find her as spellbinding and enthralling as I do and embrace the deathly dark side of Brigid known as Maman Brigitte.

Chapter 1

Maman Brigitte in Haiti

Her Name Variations

There are many variations to her name such as Maman, Maman Brigitte, Mother Brigitte, Big Brigitte, Mademoiselle Brigitte, Gran Brijit. For the purpose of the book, I will refer to her throughout as Maman Brigitte or simply as Brigitte.

Vodou in Haiti

Before I delve into this fascinating practice, I would like to reiterate that I have absolutely no personal, familial or cultural connection to Vodou in any shape or form. In fact, I have no knowledge of Haitian culture at all and have never stepped foot in Haiti. My sole reason for diving deep down into Vodouism/Voodooism is purely because of my interest in Brigid as not only as an Irish deity but also as a global icon. There are many versions of her found across the world. These include saintly versions of her in Scotland, England and Wales as well as the Goddess in England, Rome and the Caribbean. Out of all these variations of her, I found Maman Brigitte fascinating in the brief description that I had come across. Across the internet she was often described as the only red haired and white skinned Vodou deity. How did she travel so far from Ireland to the other side of the world? And how did she merge, if indeed she did, with African Vodouism/Voodooism?

As with showcasing Brigid as Goddess of Ireland it would have made zero sense to simply give a description of her without considering the cultural setting and the societal practices at the time of her origins. These are fundamental to the emergence of spiritual figures or practices. To showcase Maman Brigitte, it is also necessary to understand the history and circumstances of both Haiti and New Orleans from where she belongs, and which are not the same. Vodou is a complex religion. I am barely skimming the surface with my research and genuinely wish no disrespect to the peoples and ways of Haiti and New Orleans. I am a not a novice with Brigid, but I am a novice in her other appearances outside my own country of origin. It is my sincerest wish to showcase one of the most popular goddess manifestations in the world in all her glory. This glory extends beyond Celtic Goddess and Saint and is not restricted to the Emerald Isle or the British Isles and the Celtic world but extends to the Caribbean and the Americas.

I will endeavour to briefly set the scene as it were with both Haitian and Louisianan Vodouism/Voodooism and consider how Maman Brigitte differs or is similar in both practices. As I lift the veil of mystery surrounding her, I hope you contemplate another guise of her to whom you can call upon for specific matters in your life, most notably for all issues pertaining to the experience of death or dark issues that need recognition and healing in your life. The following chapters are historical in content and tone, but I hope you bear with me as I try to keep the facts to a minimum to help us get an image or a sense of the energies surrounding the birth of Maman Brigitte. So, get comfortable, pull up a pew and let's project ourselves to a small mountainous land formerly known as Ayiti (Haiti).

History of Haiti

Early settlers of Haiti were known as the Taino and Arawak peoples who lived here in peace until the arrival of Christopher Columbus in 1492. Upon Colombus' arrival Ayiti was renamed Hispaniola which later evolved to Haiti. Haiti is located between the Caribbean and the North Atlantic Ocean. Columbus set up settlements to mine for gold that he had noticed on the natives. Once settled the Spaniards began to marry and reproduce with

Taino women. Women had power in ancient Taino society. They were leaders and chiefs of villages. With the arrival of the Europeans women married sometimes of their own volition and sometimes forcibly. After thirty years of Spanish settlement smallpox erased the Taino from Haiti. Natives who were unsuccessful in standing up to the Spaniards were killed, sold into slavery or else escaped into the mountains and founded settlements of refuge. They were known as maroons (runaways). When the Spanish did not find gold, they shifted their attention to agriculture. By 1650 the Spanish had run out of native slaves as a result of smallpox, death through overwork or revolt. Business was booming in the cotton, sugarcane, coffee, and tobacco industries but staffing was a problem. Spain authorized the importation of new slaves from Africa to make up the difference. Slaves to Haiti specifically came from the Yoruba region in Western Africa. Central to the Yoruba religion and its people is the Mother Goddess, who I believe manifested as Maman Brigitte in Haiti as a great mother figure.

As Western Africa was where forced slavery began it is given much reverence in the practice of Haitian Vodou and is referred to as *Ginen*. The name Ginen is the traditional name of the region of West Africa, nowadays known as Benin where the earliest slaves were forcibly placed on ships headed to the New World. Benin is named after a great civilisation that developed into a huge wealthy empire that was ahead of its time in art, textiles and warfare. Many Europeans, including the Irish, travelled to Benin to buy such wares which may have resulted in some Irish getting caught up there by accident when slaves were forcibly captured and transplanted oversees. If Irish merchants were in Benin and got caught up in enforced slavery they might have been specifically chosen if they had red hair as this was seen to be quite unique. Women and men with pale skin and red hair were considered rare and therefore profitable in specific industries.

By mid-17th Century slaves had become Benin's most profitable export. Over fifteen thousand slaves were transferred to Hispaniola from other areas in the Caribbean (Tann, 2012).

Yoruba

Benin was home to the Yoruba religion which is generally regarded as the most salient surviving traditional African belief system in the New World (Fandrich, 2007) and it directly affected the emergence of Vodou in Haiti. Central to Yoruba belief is a supreme being with a host of lesser gods who work closely with humans on their behalf. The Yoruba people brought with them to Haiti spirits that they had venerated on their homeland. The spirits that they brought with them from Africa shifted and realigned in response to their needs as captives. Some spirits were forgotten whilst others were given a centrality they never had in their homeland (Brown, 2010).

In Yoruba religious practice, oral poetry is connected to religion. Poetry that exists includes praise poetry, divination poetry, poetry of ancestors and magical incantation poetry. This is reminiscent of the role poetry played in the life of Bards and Druids in Pagan Ireland when Brigid as Goddess was worshipped.

In Yoruba culture women are independent even though marriage is considered the norm. Women are strong and independent who earn their own money through trading and marketing. Marriage is seen as a means to expand their trade by bridging their existing community to the community of their husbands. These strong economic and social roles translated into political power and influence. Women served their communities as advisers, healers, priestesses, intelligence agents, entrepreneurs and chiefs. All of these characteristics would come to be seen in the persona of Maman Brigitte. Even though she speaks very little or is mute in ceremony she would come to be a spirit that protects women and pushes them to become their own person with significant power. She would also represent the essence of female strength by embodying what it means to serve her community as guardian of the cemetery, co-leader of a nation of spirits and healer.

Returning to the concept that our earliest human beginnings began as descendants from the Great African Mother, we can see many similarities in Yoruba practices and beliefs that are also to be found in the Goddess Brigid. In Yoruba, Ogun, a principal god is the divine blacksmith (Brigid is Goddess of smithcraft). He is the divinity of lightning, fire and magic and represents the principle of divine rulership. Although we cannot claim that Brigid is the divinity of lightning we certainly can for fire and magic. Oshogbo, a city in Nigeria was the Yoruba centre for art and creativity. Brigid is also connected to art and creativity and was considered the goddess of inspiration for all creative endeavours.

When the slaves from West Africa arrived, they were baptized and forced to go to church, but they received no religious education (Métraux, 2016). Despite no religious instruction, Métraux comments that

...in their belief, there is no sharp break between the religion that they practice and in which they believe, and the Catholicism to which they are bound. (Métraux, 2016).

Even with a pronounced religious tradition they openly integrated with the new Catholic religion forced upon them. In the absence of new doctrine or religious instruction in their new country of residence, Vodou took on its new character which shifted according to their new needs as slaves and also to include Catholicism.

Life in Haiti was atrocious for slaves and life expectancy was very short. With a consistent arrival of new slaves annually, indigenous African ways were constantly brought forward onto the plantations. A fresh turnover with specific religious practices enforced the continuation and practice of their faith. It can be argued that the consistently high number of African slaves forced into slavery in Haiti is what kept the emotional connection to and trust in their gods and goddesses. I can only imagine how their pleas to their ancestors and gods sounded at nighttime in the plantations as they came together after the gruelling day. Despair, rage, anguished pleas would have echoed across the land in the dead of the night.

Life was short on the plantations of Hispaniola. By 1720 eight thousand new slaves arrived annually. France soon joined in the scramble for Haiti and managed to get the western part, known as Saint Domingue, whilst the eastern Spanish side was Santa Domingo. The French pumped money into the agricultural technology and as a result had a booming trade, producing 60% of the world's coffee and 40% of its sugar.

At the time of the French Revolution there were 500,000 enslaved Africans in Haiti. There were 30,000 *gens de couleur* (mixed race of slaves and whites) and there was a paltry 20,000 white men. The whites were outnumbered. Tension was growing. Tension between the whites and slaves, between the whites and the *gens de couleur* (who were not white enough) and between the *gens de couleur* and the slaves.

Inspired by the French revolution of 1789 several meetings were held by the slaves to plan an insurrection and to take over the colony in a bid for freedom. Sheer numbers of the slaves overtook the *grands blancs* and *gens de couleur*.

It is clear that during the Revolution magico-religious beliefs served to mobilize resistance and foster a revolutionary mentality (Geggus, 1991)

In two months four thousand slave owners were killed and plantations burned. In 1804 after ten years of war, Haiti was free.

Haiti became the first independent country in the Caribbean, the first black republic to be born from a successful slave revolt and the practice of Vodou is frequently credited for its success.

Voodoo is often depicted as a unifying force that helped make possible the great uprising of 1791 (Geggus, 1991)

Haitian Vodou Principles

Haitian Vodou is where it all began and Louisianan Vodoo is where it rose and evolved into what we think we know of Vodou today. In Haitian Vodou Brigid is known as either Gran Brijit or as Manman Brijit/Manman Brigitte. In Louisianan Voodoo she is known as Maman Brigitte. I personally, feel more of a connection to her in the latter expression. Although Haitian Vodou and Louisianan Voodoo are separate they share similar traditions and I feel it's necessary to consider the original tenets of Vodou, specific to Haiti as a basis to view, once more how Gran/Manman Brijit evolved into Maman Brigitte in the New World of New Orleans.

According to Tann (2012) Vodou is essentially a family-oriented practice that is largely experienced through direct personal involvement as well as the personal practice of various rituals or ceremonies. According to Tann (2012) it is practised by millions of people every day, inside and outside of Haiti. Haitian Vodou is by all accounts a cultural and spiritual practice that adheres to no written dogma. As a result, the two most important sources for Vodou are oral tradition (this is also the case for Irish paganism) which is passed on by priestesses and priests known as mambos and oungans and direct contact with the divine beings through possession, divination, or dreams. It has evolved out of centuries of practice into what it is today.

As an Afro-Caribbean religion Vodou follows a cosmological model found in many West African religions with a creator who rules the world from afar and a host of divine intermediary spirits who oversee and control the natural world and its inhabitants. When African slaves arrived in the New World they were introduced to this concept. They then amalgamated their own divine spirits with these saints which resulted in the complex and compelling religions created to meet the pressing needs of horrific conditions on the plantations (Noonan, 2020).

Upon arrival the slaves remained faithful to the one possession they were able to bring with them, that is, their beliefs (Métraux, 2016). Although the slaves brought their indigenous ways with them from Africa, Haitian Vodouism is not essentially African Vodouism. Africa is a very large continent and the western region itself contains many different areas with unique practices. These practices arrived along with the slaves, but they blended it together for the purpose of their new-found condition as slaves.

The spelling of Vodou comes from Vodu which is also spelled Vodun. It is a word used to describe the spirits served by the West African people. Those who practice Vodou are called Vodouisants though it would appear that most practitioners prefer to say they serve the Lwa (a group of spirits in Haitian Vodou) rather than say they are a Vodouisant (Tann, 2012).

Veneration of the ancestors is at the root of this cultic, practice-oriented tradition. It is a religion inherited from their ancestors and cannot be separated from their family and community emphasis. (This was also at the heart of Irish Celtic paganism.) Vodou is a conglomeration of elements of all kinds, dominated by African traditions but also includes certain beliefs from European folklore (Métraux, 2016).

Vodou ceremonies also contain Catholic elements and imagery. (Catholic ceremonies contain pagan elements and imagery.) The core belief is in a creator divinity and a series of lesser non-human spirits given to humanity by the creator to help humanity. The universal creator is Bondye 'The Good God'. Interestingly 'The Good God' to the Irish Celts was 'The

Dagda' who is said to be the father of Brigid. The Creator or Bondye is also referred to as Gran Mèt or Great Master. Bondye created the universe and continues to create the universe daily. Bondye is considered to be the essence of love and if it is his will, things will happen or change. Although this is a monotheistic tradition it contains a polytheistic belief in many sub-gods or lesser gods. A Vodou priesthood exists and both men and women can join this priesthood which was a similar practice in the Celtic Druidic tradition.

The Lwa in Haitian Vodou

My understanding of the Lwa in Haitian Vodouism is something akin to the Catholic God and the angels. Presiding over all the universe is the central figure God and his legion of angels. In Haitian Vodouism Bondye is the ruler of fate and destiny and the embodiment of cosmic order (Tann, 2012).

The Lwa or lesser/sub gods work for Bondye keeping the universe ticking over and interceding on the behalf of those who serve them. There are hundreds of thousands of Lwa. Some are Taino, some from Africa, Europe and other parts of the Western Hemisphere and Asia. Some Lwa were discovered on the island of Haiti, others came with slaves, visitors, immigrants. Some were once human beings and/or Catholic Saints.

Each person has a personal Lwa (much like the Catholic Guardian Angel or Spiritual Door-Keeper). In addition to a personal Lwa each person has a Lwa of ancestry, geographical location, family, initiation lineage (if priest or priestess) or even a random Lwa that they might come to encounter in various ways (Tann, 2012). As each person has a personal Lwa like a guardian angel they are intimately connected with each individual. The Lwa is considered to have been part of a person's life since birth and once the person knows the identity of the Lwa, the Lwa can work with and for a person in ways that other Lwa cannot. This dominant Lwa is called master of the head. They gather around the head of a living human, like the halo of a Catholic saint and this Lwa stays the closest to that person to make sure they remain healthy, happy and safe (Tann, 2012). It is clear there is a reverence for the head if this particular Lwa is called master of the head. Like in Celtic Ireland the head was considered extremely sacred. People are encouraged to keep their Masters of the head a secret for fear they can be corrupted to talk them into doing or do them harm (Tann, 2012).

The Lwa are served in ceremony after Bondye has been acknowledged. For the most part, ceremony is the way the Lwa can be accessed for information or help on matters in everyday life or in planning a revolution! Regardless of how the ceremony may appear the only one being worshipped is Bondye and not the Lwa. The role of the Lwa is to work on behalf of Bondye on everyday matters that are important to humans. Each Lwa has specific requirements for service, including songs, dances, colours and preferred offerings. Nations of Lwa can be classified into three major nations – Rada, Petro/Petwo, and Gede. Brigitte belongs to and presides over the Gede Lwa with her partner, Baron Samedi.

The Rada Lwa means 'root'. These were the original slaves that were brought to Haiti. They form the basis of Vodou heritage. They embody ancestral emphasis. They preserve and celebrate a peaceful way of life before slavery.

The Petro Lwa are the warrior tribes and are what appear to be the muse of Hollywood's depiction of wild, fierce almost savage like acts in ceremony. They stand for strength, violence and force in the face of treachery and slavery.

The Gede Lwa concern themselves with death and as said before it is to this family that Maman Brigitte belongs. Her area of concern is death. Death is trifold in Haiti. (The number three is also associated with Brigid). When a person dies in Haiti they will have a funeral, be buried, and be remembered by their family. If the deceased is a Vodouisant they will be ritually honoured twice after death. Once, not long after death at the Dessounin ceremony and once more at the Kase-Kanari 'breaking of pots' ceremony that brings their spirit out from under the water. (Water in Irish Celtic belief was considered a feminine energy.) It is here where the deceased rests with Mèt Agwe for a year and a day (which is also a significant time frame in Celtic Irish mythology) and then the Kase-Kanari elevates it to Ginen with the blessed ancestors who have gone before.

If for some reason the deceased is not a Vodouisant or their successors refuse to honour them, their souls go underwater and is never reclaimed. Rather than being condemned to wander between this life and the next, two very special Lwa gather up forgotten or lost souls and give them new purpose as the Gede Lwa, an incremental horde of the dead. These two Lwa are Maman Brigitte and her 'husband' Baron Samedi, the mother and father of the Gede Lwa. This made a huge impact on me when I first learned this about Manman Brigitte. Across continents she is the same maternal essence. She is mother to *all* the living and *all* the dead.

The Gede Lwa

The bosses of the Gede, if you like, are Brigitte and Baron. The Gede Lwa are closer to us as humans than any other Lwa so they have a special concern for life and all things earthly. They loved life's pleasures, and they miss them in their different spiritual state. In ceremony, after Bondye, Papa Legba (Hekate/Peter of the Keys) is asked to open 'the gates' to experience him and/or any other Lwa. The Gede Lwa ar the only Lwa in Haitian Vodou that anyone can serve. They are accessible to all. This sounds familiar as Brigid who is accessible to all as Catholic Saint or Goddess and possessed extreme charitable qualities.

The Gede Lwa are said to be very funny in ceremony as they steal food, mimic intercourse, crack jokes (Tann, 2012). They are also asked to help a woman become pregnant or offer their advice on how to heal a sick child. This also echoes Saint Ffraid of Scotland and Brigid of Ireland as both the Goddess and Saint. The Gede Lwa are generally called at the end of a ceremony. Described as gate crashers, attempting to hijack a ceremony by leading those present in catchy, bawdy songs (Tann, 2012). The Gede Lwa also have a sexual nature. These Lwa are known to use vulgar words and make sexual puns and comments, to dance the Banda (a dance that is an uncanny mimicry of the motions of human intercourse and to carry around a phallus–shaped baton). Although they appear to be vulgar, they are harmless. They never curse or harm anyone. They can no longer have sex as they are dead, but they mimic it to entertain and to remind their children that life and death are one. Sex is the ultimate expression of the very essence of life. In death there is nothing to fear. It is simply an end of one state and a beginning of another. The Gede Lwa push boundaries of good taste and behaviour. They remind us of the beauty of life. Specific in Haitian culture and all the suffering that was part and parcel of their lives the Gede remind us of the beauty that can also be found in life and that is independent of materialism. Haitian Vodou is the ceremonial service of the Lwa. This is when deities such as Maman Brigitte or the Baron come into possession to speak to all those who have congregated. It appears that Maman Brigitte is rarely seen in possession or ceremony. Maybe this has something to do with her muted presence? If the Gede rulers appear in ceremony it is said that her partner the Baron Samedi/Baron Yo makes a strong entrance. However, I have come across one author, Lilith Dorsey, who witnessed Brigitte in possession and wrote about it in her book *Orishas, Goddesses, And Voodoo Queens.*

Maman Brigitte in Haitian Vodou
Maman Brigitte and her partner are the couple of the Gede. They are an item and come as a package. Therefore, I think it is

necessary to give a short overview of the Bawon/Baron as well as Maman Brigitte. Understanding what they look like, why they are invoked in ceremony, what house, or family they belong to and what is generally offered to them can help us get a feel for their specific type of energy. This energy can help us connect more easily to them for very specific issues. For example, Brigid as Goddess whom I will call upon for inspiration for anything connected to words in any shape or form is very different for me from Brigitte whom I will call upon for the heavy stuff and by heavy stuff I mean deep rooted fear, anxiety, depression, ancestral trauma, upheaval, chaos, complete overhaul in life and fears specifically connected to death. These belong in her domain. Once we understand the circumstances surrounding her birth in Haitian Vodou and how she very much evolved in the New World we can see how the people in both Haiti and New Orleans were going through immensely deep, dark, traumatic life events. Their need was so strong for a specific guide, for a being to whom they could relate, to whom they could plead for help and to whom they could turn, as in the case of Haitian slaves, to overthrow their suppressors. In the New World their need was for a deity who would mother and nurture them as they transitioned into a new life far away from all that was previously familiar but who would also push them to bring out their survival instincts to stay alive in a new country and thrive whilst also enjoying basic earthly pleasures. Although she was and continues to be a mother figure in new situations, she is a tough mother that pushes you beyond what you perceive your capabilities to be.

Baron – Yo

Baron Samedi is the partner or husband of Maman Brigitte. Baron is the title given to various powerful Gedes and specifically to Baron Samedi. In Haitian culture his name is spelled Bawon Samdi. (This is somewhat similar to the title 'Brig' in Brigid.

Brig is the honourific title of goddess.) Bawon Samdi is most associated with death and the dead (Noonan, 2010). He resides in the cemetery. The large central cross is found in every Haitian cemetery (Noonan, 2010). It symbolises the intersection of this world and the otherworld and is sacred to him. The first male buried in every cemetery is dedicated to him.

The Baron Lwa are readers and judges of the dead. With these, the dead is not the ancestors but the forgotten ones, the unknown. This is hugely significant as I have previously said. Brigid as Saint is connected to all those on the fringes of society, the outcasts, the forgotten. All of these souls lingering and lost between worlds are gathered by the Barons and they are brought into the nation of the Gede. The Gede relate to death and sex.

Gede is the stark reality of death, as well as the life-affirming powers of sex, and as lord of these two realms which all mortals must face, he is a humourous yet confronting spirit that peels away the veneer of civilized manners and hypocrisy (Noonan, 2010).

Baron Samedi is dressed in a black suit and top hat. He wears dark glasses to protect himself from the light of day or with one lens broken to demonstrate that he can see in both worlds. His colours are purple and black. His food is spicier than humans can stand. His cigarettes are strong and unfiltered. His favourite drink is spicey rum. All his images contain skulls or crosses. He is sometimes depicted with Archangel Gabriel. Although the Gede represent death, Baron himself represents judgement and control over death. Baron may not actually kill a man, but he can give the order for a man to live or die by withholding or giving permission 'to dig his grave'. While some forms of Baron can speak, some simply lay still on the ground or floor (in ceremony) or can only speak once their jaws have been tied shut with cotton gauze, as was once done to corpses before embalming as we know it today. For some, in Haitian

Vodou, it appears that Baron is the master and Brigitte (who goes by many names) is inferior to him. For others, Brigitte is his counterpart and yet for others she is his superior.

Manman Brijit

Researching Maman Brigitte has been difficult to source verifiable evidence. My journey took me to scholarly articles and historical archives and also to YouTube in an attempt to glean as much information as possible about her. In many articles or books, I disappointingly came across sections with information on her running for little more than one line at the minimum to a paragraph at the most but I found enough to get me started in understanding this wonderful dark goddess.

Baron's consort/partner/wife is named Brijiit after the honourific given to very old or respectable women. In Haitian Vodou she is also known as Grande Brigitte, Maman Brigitte, Gran Boujitte or Gran Brijit. By some accounts Gran Brijit is said to be different from Maman Brijiit. In an interesting YouTube episode titled *Manman Brigitte Rebirth Goddess order* by X-LAB TV she speaks of the role women played in the Haitian revolution in brothels. She speaks of the Mama Brigitte society which was a cult of girls in close proximity to slave masters. As the Brothel was a gateway for information these working girls were instrumental in relaying information that helped bring a successful outcome for Haitians in the Haitian revolution. At the head of this Bouzen society was Gran Brigit. She is described as a figure who is now 'past it' but caters to the health and wellbeing of the working girls in her care. She is said to be reserved and motherly but at the same time, the boss. She has done the job in the past, has experience to share but has stepped back to give way to the younger girls. Although this is very interesting, I could not find any literature to back this up.

Noonan (2010) writes that Manman Brijit she is often depicted as an old, asexual woman who is said to be mute and dressed like a corpse when she comes in possession in ritual. McCarthy Brown (2010) concurs with this representation of her and describes her as 'an ancient, hobbled woman who can barely walk or talk'. McCarthy also writes that possession by Maman Brigitte are infrequent.

The realm of Maman Brigitte is also the cemetery where she, along with her partner are said to dominate. The graves under her special protection are said to be marked with a mound of stones (Deren, 1970). With her partner she is the Lwa of Life and Death. As she and he belong to both realms, they are in fact, eternal and this gives them the liberty to say and do as they please, which might explain their associated outlandish and crude behaviour.

Conflicting this narrative of her as old woman comes from several established writers in the world of Voodoo who describe her as a very sexual being. Laguerre is an expert in the field of Haitian Vodou who describes her as formerly a ritual prostitute who used to dance the Banda for Bawon. From their union were born all the other Gedes, their children. She is said to be a former prostitute who had numerous children with her husband/partner Bawon Samdi (Noonan, 2010). Laguerre says that Brijit is one of the most important members of the Gede family.

In Vodou rituals her image in art or on sequenced flags varies from a stately woman in purple to a lamia-like figure with a split tail to a provocatively posed young woman with legs wide open reminiscent of Sheela na Gig, (Noonan, 2010).

Artist André Pierre paints Brigitte as dark-skinned, wearing a purple and black outfit with a skirt wrapped in a very snake-like way, around her lower body. The serpent is one of the oldest symbols of the Goddess, depicting fertility, rebirth and immortality and is closely associated with the Goddess Brigid and the Great African Mother, Isis. In Pierre's creation Manman Brijit is not very old and has black hair done in a high hair do. Behind the top of her hairdo are flames. This is highly suggestive of Brigid, who is considered a solar Goddess and as Saint in one of her myths is said to have fire coming from her head. He compares Bawon Samedi to Adam and Gran Brijit to Eve which as Noonan (2010) says if she is compared to Eve then she is 'the mother of all the living and the dead'. Eve is also linked to sin and sexual temptation which might explain the sexual facet to Maman Brigitte. It could also be a subtle middle finger to the behaviour of nice girls encouraged by the patriarchy. Another artist by the name of Pierre Joseph Valcin has her in a very snake-like dress and instead of a high hairdo, she has a conical purple hat. I, personally, see the height coming from the head as an ability to connect to the higher realm and to be gifted with high intellect which for me is a nod in the direction of the Irish Goddess Brigid who is associated with all matters 'high' such as intellect, celestial connection etc.

Although she has been linked to Eve, Sheela na Gig and even to Mary Magdalene, she seems to be specifically linked to the Yoruba Orisa Oya and the Irish Catholic Saint Brigid of Kildare (Noonan, 2010). Looking at the characteristics of both Oya and Brigid, I definitely see a unique and beautiful blend of these two deities who I believe evolved into Maman Brigitte energy very much centred on women and their suffering during the slave trade and later on, emigration. I also believe Maman Brigitte contains elements of the group of female Lwa called the Ezili, especially as Maman Brigitte is often portrayed as silent or with her mouth taped. I contemplated the meaning of her silence in comparison to Brigid's poetic qualities.

Could Brigitte represent the silenced woman, found across many cultures, especially as we have seen and will see in Haitian and Irish women? Could it be a sign of power, that no words are necessary, actions speak louder? Could this simply be an old representation of her in her homeland, one that is nonetheless a part of her, even when she travels to the New

World? On new soil, her silenced past might transform itself into her power. We'll see!

So, who are the Ezili whose traits are also seen in Brigitte? They are a group of female spirits in Haitian Vodou and are sometimes said to be reflections of the Virgin Mary in Catholicism. They are different to the Virgin Mary; in that they are said to be closer to the human day to day drama. When called upon they provide examples of love, care and hard work. As well as all the positive qualities they possess they also model anger and righteousness, rage and power, sensuality, sexuality, fear, frustration, need and loneliness. In so doing, they become mirrors that reflect what would otherwise remain, as it were, in so many cultures, women's silent and unhonoured pain.

In Haitian history Ezili Danto, the great Mother is said to have fought fiercely beside her children in the Haitian slave revolution. She is said to bear scars on her cheek from wounding in battle but interestingly, she also had her tongue cut out, rendering her speechless. This is said to have been done by her own people who could not trust her to guard their secrets. When Ezili Danto possesses someone, she cannot speak. She is said to utter a sound such as dey-dey dey or k-k-k. Danto is viewed as a powerful protector of women and defender of women. She is patron of LGBTQ individuals and abused women and children. Her energy is likened to a stern mother and a strict disciplinarian.

Poor Haitian women in Haiti and in the USA assume that the children born to them belong to them and are their sole responsibility. For them, the physical, social, and economic risks of having children explain the occurrence of a condition called pa-pale (pas parler/not-speaking disease). Although it can befall others who have reasons for depression, pa-pale is said to be found most often among women who have just given birth. Such women take to their beds and literally do not speak, sometimes for months at a time. Like the mute Ezili Danto, they have had their voices taken from them by the people closest to them. As I've already said, I find the muted aspect of Maman Brigitte fascinating and have somewhat traced this back to Ezili Danto, whether I'm right or wrong, I don't know. However, as a champion of women and being speechless, I very much see an element of her in the personality of Brigitte. I also feel her maternal approach is fiercer than nurturing. If Brigitte can be viewed (in my opinion) as a holy trinity of the Ezili, Oya and Brigid we can possibly feel the difference in the motherly energy of Ezili Danto and Brigid. To me they are very different and quite tilted into a category of hard mother or soft mother. But when they come together in Brigitte, she is the combined ferocity and gentleness making her such an empowering mother figure. Brigitte is also said to contain aspects of Oya, the Yoruban Goddess of wind and air.

Oya

Among the Yoruba region there exists a female divinity called Oya. She is referred to as the goddess of the river Niger that is said to contain her very spirit. As a river she brings movement and opportunity with every twist and turn. In addition to the element of water she also possesses the properties of wind and air. Oya is described as great and powerful. She is the embodiment of change just like strong winds bringing about huge clearings and change. Little wonder that this energy is part of the dynamic of Brigitte. Oya is also said to be the owner of the marketplace and the commerce that occurs there. In the old and New World, the marketplace for women was highly important as a means to earn their own money and for women to come together as a community. As well as Oya, Brigid of Ireland is also said to be a feature in the character of Maman Brigitte.

Brigid of Ireland

Marcelin (1949) is the one that links Maman Brigitte to Saint Brigid. It is, for me, impossible to briefly narrate information about Ireland's most powerful Saint and not emphasize the Goddess Brigid (I spell both the Goddess and the Saint as Brigid).

In Celtic Ireland, Brigid was one Great Mother Goddess. Like other Mother Goddesses in Ireland, she was inseparably linked to the land. However, she did not remain solely exclusive to one territory, but rather she transcended all territories. Brigid was the Triple Goddess of Healing, Poetry and Smithcraft. Her father was the good god An Dagda who was the God of the Otherworld. As such she was able to traverse both worlds easily. As Goddess, her partner was Bres. She had one son Ruadan who was killed. With his death she is said to have voiced her lament into what became known as keening. Keening is a soulful wail to express and release grief. She was also said to escort souls to the Otherworld in death. Her feast day is at Imbolc, the start of the Celtic Spring. It is believed that at this point of the year she breathes new life into the dead mouth of winter (Condren, 1989). As Great Mother Goddess she embodies maternal imagery in how she provides incessantly for all inhabitants on earth, through her body the earth. She is closely associated with the cow who is also considered a nurturing animal.

This maternal imagery continues into the life of Saint Brigid of Kildare. Brigid is depicted as exceptionally generous, kind, and compassionate to the poor. There are many myths about Brigid that show her great compassion and nurturing nature to everyone. There are also many myths about Brigid of Kildare that show an otherworldly, mischievous side that mimics the energy of the Otherworld. This is always done with the intention to be hospitable or to be charitable to either guests or to the poor. Both the Goddess and Saint are connected to the element of Fire and are both illustrated with flames coming from the head.

As Saint she had a reputation for academic excellence as well as teaching and healing. Brigid established the first nunnery in Ireland that was a community composed of both monks and nuns. Many people visited here to learn and to avail of healing. She was treated not only as an equal in the Catholic church but also became the only female Bishop. Brigid is known as *Muire na nGael*, meaning Mary of the Gael.

For me, the Goddess and the Saint are intertwined. Much of Saint Brigid's miraculous feats and attributes have too many similarities to the Goddess Brigid to be a separate being. This interplay of the Goddess/Saint Brigid continues, in my opinion to the interplay of energies between the triple energies of, Ezili Danto, the Yoruba Goddess Oya and Brigid. This trio *may* have fused together to become Maman Brigitte.

I see many similarities between the Goddess Brigid and Maman Brigitte. Both Brigid and Maman Brigitte are served by Priestesses and Priests. Both have been blended with Catholicism. Both are available and are especially invoked for all those on the fringes of society. Both are invoked especially for and by women. They both have a partner. Both are blended versions of themselves. I believe Saint Brigid to have come from the Goddess and I believe Maman Brigitte to come from both Goddess/Saint Brigid and the African Goddess Oya as well as, possibly, Ezili Danto. Both represent blended peoples. Both are linked to fire: Brigid as Goddess of fire and Maman Brigitte with her fiery peppers in her rum. Both like a tipple; Brigid is connected to ale, Brigitte with rum. Both represent death and rebirth even if one is more dominant in one than the other. Maman Brigitte represents death that is inevitable if there is to be rebirth and Brigid is the rebirth after death. Brigid was also psychopomp in Celtic mythology, who overshadowed departed souls to the afterlife. It was a small connection to death in comparison to Maman Brigitte, but the connection to death is still there. Brigid represents new life at Imbolc. Maman Brigitte also symbolised new life through displacement and emigration in New Orleans. This may be forced and unwanted, but it still can be considered a rebirth. She too had new life breathed into her, allowing her to develop in the Deep South. For life and death with Brigid and Maman Brigitte, I very much sense the figure eight. Both influence and reinforce each other or arguably different sides of the same coin. They are each connected to life and death but have their area of speciality in their unique part of the world. Both the Goddess Brigid and Maman Brigitte are connected to communication, Brigid as Goddess of oration and Maman Brigitte for possibly repressed communication. Both are venerated at Samhain in both cultures. Both Brigid and Maman Brigitte are nurturing to lost souls whether they wander aimlessly in life or death and I feel both Brigid and Maman Brigitte are especially for women and all who identify as women.

Marcelin portrays Maman Brigitte as very old but equally as powerful as her husband. He says in possession she lies like a dead person, and the others bind her jaw with a black scarf, sealing her ears and nose with cotton, and covering her with a white cloth while spraying her with white rum. She never speaks and is still when she comes in possession.

If Maman Brigitte was birthed into the Haitian experience of slavery was there an Irish presence there or did an Irish presence come from Africa along with the Yoruba tradition? There seems to be no historical evidence of Irish presence in the Caribbean from the 17th to the 19th century, but large numbers of Irish were sold as indentured servants to America and the West Indies in the mid-1600s as part of Cromwell's reign. Servant traders presented the West Indies to the Irish poor as an area of great economic opportunity. Servants received the cost of their passage and food, clothing, and shelter on the plantation in return for up to seven years of contracted labour.

The Irish poor were more willing to seek opportunities in the West Indies than their British counterparts because of high food shortages, high unemployment, and English military disruption in Ireland. Colonial Servitude in the Anglo-Caribbean was temporary and non-hereditary, with legal personhood, while slavery was permanent, hereditary with sub-human legal status (Reilly, 2016). The terms servants refer to Europeans whilst slavery refers to persons of colour. Although both servants and slaves were at times unfree and forced into 'service', indentured servants had some rights whereas slaves did not. In Europe, some prisoners of war or political prisoners were sent to places like the Caribbean against their will and without a predetermined period of servitude. When they arrived, they were required to serve their master who purchased their labour for a limited number of years, depending on their age. Many didn't live to see the end of their service because of barbaric treatment, climatic conditions and harsh work conditions. Irish servitude was temporary slavery (Reilly, 2016). Indentured servants of Ireland were described as restless and insubordinate as they realised that their longed-for material advancement most probably wasn't going to happen. This was said to be rife amongst indentured servants but particularly troublesome were the Irish (Beckles, 1990).

Ireland played her part in the Atlantic Economy by sending over food, most notably meat, herrings, and butter to feed the slaves. These foods were highly preserved in order to last in a hot climate. For Saint Domingue in particular herring and beef were sent. Limerick as a port packed six vessels annually for the Guinea and slave coasts as well as the Indian islands (Rodgers, 2000). With such a part in the Atlantic Economy it is highly probable that many Irish travelled to the West Indies on board these ships and had cause to either get caught up in the business of slave plantations or voluntarily stay to work alongside the slaveowners on the plantations.

Others went to the Caribbean as members of various European navies. Irish sailors and soldiers fought for France and England on the Caribbean. Priests from Brittany (the Celtic province of France) were present in Haiti before its independence in 1804. Catholics in both Brittany and Ireland were devoted to Brigid.

The influence of Irish settlers and sailors and Breton priests in spreading knowledge of Saint Brigid in Haiti cannot be overstated (Noonan, 2010).

Food offerings to Manman Brijiit in Haitian Vodou include potatoes (you can't get more Irish), plantains, corn, grilled pistachios and cane syrup are appropriate food offerings for Gran Brigitte as well as salted herring (which was intentionally imported from Ireland), dried cod and white rum which was the food of Irish sailors.

In other contexts, she comes as an ancient, hobbled woman who can barely walk or talk. Gran Brijit (Grand-mother Brijit), as she is usually called, is an old woman who no longer has sexual power. Papa Gede's enlivening sexual energy, his infectious humour and telling satire, his childlike disregard for social control has no parallels in Gran Brijit. Gede's domination of the realm of the dead reflects a time when male ancestors, as well as living males, held all the power in Haitian families (Brown, 2010). This could be why she is depicted as silent. This could possibly explain how Gran/Manman Brijit is somewhat different in Haiti as to how she is in Louisiana. In the New World as a means of survival, women would have to find their own voices and in doing so, they would start a new tradition and generation of female empowerment. Possibly it was the empowered, independent Yoruba feminine energy that was brought into Haiti that served as a role model for Haitian women who, in turn would bring that energy to the New World and let it flourish. According to Noonan (2010)

> *Gran Brijit is a cultural assemblage, created by people in Haiti under the conditions of cultural contact, slavery, oppression, creativity, freedom from the Catholic church for over fifty years and a spiritual aesthetic that valued the incorporation of new elements. The religious practices of Ireland in the 16th to the 19th centuries may not have been as foreign to an African worldview as it might appear, and the blending of traditions that created Gran Brijit may not have been such a difficult chore. The meeting of Oya and Saint Brigit was the birth of Gran Brijit, who then took on a life of her own, as deities-especially those who appear in possession – usually do.*

It has been necessary to look at Haiti from a spiritual and historical perspective as over 10,000 Haitians landed on the swampy soil of Louisiana in 1809 following the Haitian revolution and with them, they brought this specific type of Vodou to the Americas. In New Orleans where Voodoo was already practised, Haitian Vodou would make a significant impact. And it is possibly thanks to the substantial arrival of Haitian immigrants to New Orleans with a strongly embedded concrete practice of Vodou that we, on the other side of the world have even heard of Vodou. The Haitian people brought Vodou to the world and within that practice was a small part of Irish culture and belief in the form of Brigid. If Maman Brigitte really evolved from Oya and Brigid and was perhaps influenced by Ezili Danto, then she would continue to evolve in New Orleans to become a similar but different deity, who found herself on different territory in a different time summoned by her devotees for specific help once they reached the shores of America.

Chapter 2

Maman Brigitte in Louisiana

Voodoo in New Orleans

By the time Haitians arrived in Louisiana, Africans had already settled there for almost a century because of the slave trade from 1500–1900 and had developed their neo-African counterculture religion (Fandrich, 2007). Between 1717 and 1721 more than 2,000 Africans were brought to the French colony of Louisiana. In 1724 under French law, every aspect of enslaved or free African people could be governed in French territories. New Orleans African population was not from Yoruba but were mostly Senegalese who were taken into the Louisiana-bound slave trade. As we saw in the previous chapter, Haitian Vodou had an elaborate system of Lwa. This was not the case in Louisianan Voodoo. Louisiana lost its spiritual complexity and had hardly any African divinities. In Louisiana, Voodoo couldn't flourish the same way that it did in Haiti. In New Orleans there was a higher white-to-black population and there existed a stricter social system. After the Haitian influx of more than 10,000 immigrants, Voodoo boomed and experienced its peak pre civil war. The Haitians had brought their strongly identified practice with them, and this merged with the current practice in place in New Orleans. What was also a contributing factor to the peak in Voodoo was the waves of Irish immigrants arriving in New Orleans and bringing their strong Catholic faith with them that included Saint Brigid. The two simultaneous streams of religious and spiritual practices would blow on the smouldering fire embers in New Orleans and spark up a new peak in the interest and practice of Voodoo in the Deep South.

In Louisiana, Voodoo appealed to those superstitiously inclined, both slave and free, who were denied educational and religious opportunities and limited in their means of retribution for the many injustices they suffered (Touchstone, 1972). Folk contacted Voodoo practitioners for folk remedies, hexes and wonder or evil working amulets called *gris gris*.

A significant difference between the two similar traditions of Haitian and Louisianan Voodoo is that Louisianan Voodoo is mostly considered to be under the sphere of women (Osbey, 2011). So, here it was and possibly remains a mother-centred practice. This is where it gets interesting for me concerning Brigid. Irish people had lived in a matrifocal society where the Goddess was worshipped until the arrival of Christianity. Despite the gradual sweep over to a monotheistic faith of the one male God, the sacred feminine in the forms of the Virgin Mary and Brigid remained in the hearts of Irish folk. According to Osbey (2011) the religion in New Orleans is entirely under the remit of women who are called 'Mothers'. Interesting then, that Brigitte is Maman Brigitte or Mother Brigid.

Osbey (2011) reiterates that New Orleans is not Yoruba based Voodoo. It doesn't rely on the intercession of multiple lesser deities, nor requires that African deities be 'masqued' in the guise of Catholic Saints.

It is the ancestors who are at the heart of the Religion and true focus of our attention because of their proximity to us. They were once not only human but also our kin Osbey (2011).

The *Immigrés* of New Orleans found a very different social life when they landed in New Orleans. They found themselves having to find work in their new-found freedom to support themselves and they had to face much mistrust and fear about their cultic practice that overthrew the white man and abolished slavery in Haiti. White supremacists regarded Voodoo as a real and a symbolic threat of Negro domination (Gordon, 2012). The potential of the religion shook the foundation of white supremacy and patriarchy. The USA was the largest slaveholding country in the world having a slave population of 900,000 in a total population of 5.3 million. Voodoo was feared because of its connections to black conspiracy and slave insurrection, and specifically in New Orleans, it's powerful women of colour. I love this! I love how women of colour had become something to be feared. Free women of colour dominated Voodoo leadership in New Orleans throughout the 19th century. Queens like Betsey Toledano, Sanité Dédé and the famous Marie Laveau conducted very profitable businesses in female-centred spaces occupied by women of varied social classes and racial designation. The entrepreneurial spirit of Maman Brigitte, possibly from the Oya or Ezili Danto personalities was shining through her women here.

When thousands of Haitian *immigrés* arrived in New Orleans in 1809 the mayor tried to control slave conspiracies by allocating Congo Square formerly as *'Place Publique'* as the sole place for slave gatherings. Here they could come together to practice their traditions but in addition to that, a careful eye could be placed over them. On Sunday afternoons American African slaves could assemble to dance, sing, and remember their heritage. Food and drink were sold and soon these spectacles became a tourist attraction that lasted until 1862. Slaves were forbidden to congregate in any other part of the city. Congo Square was a focal point of subculture of New Orleans black slaves who led a lifestyle as close as possible to what they had lived in Africa. It is said that music and dance are the last characteristics of a culture to be suppressed (Donaldson, 1984). Dance, as mentioned earlier, in particular the banda dance that is suggestive of sexual intercourse is often used to honour Maman Brigitte.

Undoubtedly the mass immigration of Haitians had a huge impact on the Voodoo practices already present in New Orleans. They were in fact bringing into the city a new reality, one that was demonstrative of the empowered woman of colour, but the three waves of Irish immigrants that brought their beloved Brigid with them to the Crescent city also had an impact on Voodoo practice.

History of New Orleans

The history of New Orleans is as complex as the city itself. No stranger to colonialism (like Haiti and Ireland) the city has a rich cultural past which might explain the very 'blended' feel of the 'Big Easy'. As far back as 10.000 BC Louisiana was populated by American Indian peoples. In 1682 the French explorer La Salle claimed Louisiana for the Sun King, Louis XIV. A French settlement was established in 1718 and in 1720 the first ship of enslaved people arrived in New Orleans.

From 1724 Louisiana used the French *Code Noir* based on regulations already in force in the French territories of the Caribbean. For almost 163 years Louisianan law gave permission to slave owners to compel productive labour and use force if necessary.

Under the Treaty of Paris in 1763 France yielded Louisiana and New Orleans to Spain. In under 40 years, Louisiana and New Orleans were handed back to France in 1800. Imagine for some people at that time this meant waking up one morning to assume Spanish identity, language and culture, then reverting back to French identity, language and culture. And then in 1803, a mere three years later under the Louisianan Purchase, the state sold to the USA. Louisiana and New Orleans are now American. In forty years three different 'powers' had exerted their influence onto the city. Under American status, the Louisianan state fared very well. And this was mostly due to the free labour market in the slaves. The Louisianan state was divided into north and south. The north of the state was home to protestants from the English, German and Scots Irish persuasion whilst the south was home to Catholics because of French and Spanish influences.

In 1812 the first steamboat arrived, and the USA declared war on Britain. The British were defeated in 1815. As Louisiana became more Americanised there was a boom in commercialised sugar and cotton. New Orleans soon becomes the world's largest cotton market. This was mainly due to the service provided by the Mississippi river not to mention the free labour market of slaves in lawful existence. In 1811, 500 slaves attempted to take over the city in New Orleans, but this was unsuccessful. Increased vigilance on slaves then became necessary to prevent a similar event happening in New Orleans as happened in Haiti. Although the boom brought great economic prosperity to New Orleans, it was short lived. The Civil War of 1861–1865 ended the city's prosperity. All the plantations were destroyed. In the Reconstruction era that followed, slavery was abolished, citizenship for black men with equal protection was guaranteed and all males, regardless of race or colour were permitted to vote. This lasted for a mere 10 years. After just a decade, however, federal troops withdrew, and local whites assumed rule. For 20 years all that people of colour had been given, were taken away. The Jim Crow Laws came into force and acted as guidelines between 1890–1965 for race relations all over the United States. The laws were more prominent in eleven former confederate states where the black population and history of slavery was higher.

Jim Crow was slang for black men, and it stood for any state law passed in the south that legally segregated white and black people. Jim Crow laws were based on white supremacy and were a reaction to the Reconstruction era that came out of fear losing jobs to free men of colour. These laws attempted to 'solve the 'problem' of the black intruder in an exclusive white society'

(McLaughlin – Stonham, 2020). These conditions would be endured until the second world war where the bridge between white supremacy in the USA and Hitler's master race was too big to be ignored. Through all of this, Brigitte as dark mother would bear witness to the suffering, segregation, restriction and bias and come to be a beacon of hope for freedom.

The Irish in New Orleans

What the Irish were bringing to the New World and what they were leaving behind in Ireland is quite significant to the society they contributed to when they reached America. It was within this society that Maman Brigitte gathered momentum in her rise and popularity. When the Irish arrived, the planters to whom they were indentured paid the captain for their transportation. They were discouraged from fraternising with the black slaves. They were to face serious consequences if they absconded with black slaves. If found guilty of misalliance they could get an additional seven years added to their service.

The Irish came to New Orleans primarily for the economic opportunities associated with the thriving port city but also because it was predominantly Catholic. Upon arrival, they came together, and forged strong cohesive neighbourhoods centred on local churches that were financed and built by their communities. The first wave of Irish Immigrants to go to New Orleans was in 1798. In this year Ireland staged an uprising against British rule but failed. Rather than face continued persecution many left in the hope of finding better living conditions in the Crescent city. The trip was expensive so those that left were wealthy rather than poor. Spanish Louisiana (1763–1800) offered Irish Immigrants the opportunity to become prosperous landowners, enslavers, and merchants (Regan, 2022). When they landed, they married local creoles and found jobs in finance, health, education as well as in journalism as well as some establishing themselves as enslavers. The failed uprising and the Act of Union in 1800 saw new Irish immigrants arriving that were both Catholic and Protestant with well-developed politicised views of Ireland and a strong sense of Irish identity. The Irish found their brethren in the Americans against their common enemy – Britain. America and Britain would go to war in 1812 and America would be victorious against Britain in 1815. (Kelley, 2014)

For some Irish immigrants the profits extracted from slavery created the possibility to accumulate immense wealth. These Irish immigrants took advantage of enslaved people. They readily took to owning slaves and were confident in their innate whiteness and ability to operate plantations (Regan, 2022). From 1820–1845 over a million mostly Catholic Irish left for the USA. A population explosion, along with a major switch in agriculture from tillage to pasture, limiting tenant holdings, and sizeably reducing them, sectarian violence, faction fights, agitations against rents, tithes and labourers' wages and employment shortages outside of agriculture nudged people to seek a better life in the New World arrived in Louisiana (McCaffrey, 2004).

The cotton boom reduced transatlantic shipping rates which made travel to America all the cheaper. Because they possessed funds to emigrate, early emigrants did not represent the most impoverished Catholics, but in comparison to others leaving western Europe at that time they were poorer and less vocationally skilled. They went to cities and towns. They began work at the bottom rung of the American workforce. Men dug canals, laid railroad tracks, mined coal, copper, silver, and gold, cleaned stables, drove horses and laid building foundations. Women worked as domestics or in textile mills and shoe factories.

Arriving in New Orleans was like arriving at a brand-new world. This place offered living conditions never possible before to the Irish. Through hard work economic prosperity was not only a possibility but a high probability. Here there was an abundance of jobs, high wages, better housing conditions, plentiful food, and the familiar religion of Catholicism. When they landed, they set to work on establishing their availability for work, often at the expense of the free black people of colour. In the 1830s the business of transporting goods to and from the ship warehouses was controlled by free people of colour. Within ten years, the Irish had taken over by sheer force. They were seen to be opportunists, clannish and had representations in every field. They, like in their indentured service days, were seen to be difficult.

The third wave of Irish Immigrants was a result of the Irish potato famine in 1845 which lasted until 1849. For almost a decade about a million and a half victims sought shelter from hunger, disease, and poverty in America. After the famine in Ireland living standards and conditions significantly improved. Housing conditions improved, national schools taught young people how to read and write. As a result of a population decline there was more land available. However, parents still raised their children for export. What was known as 'The American wake' saw relatives and friends say final goodbyes to those leaving. By the end of the 19th century nearly all Irish Immigrants could read and write. The arrival of new, disadvantaged immigrants from eastern and southern Europe, lifted many Irish from the ranks of unskilled to skilled labourers and some entered the middle class. The grass on the other side did in fact seem greener. And this good life was to be preserved at all costs. With the abolition of slavery after the Civil war there was an increase in competition for jobs in an oversupplied labour market. This would result in lower wages. The Irish wanted to preserve the south. They had spent the last ten to twenty years rebirthing themselves on new territory. They had established strong, supportive communities, availed of good quality education offered by the nuns and, for the most part they were progressing economically and socially.

After the war, however, the good times were over. The south entered a period of economic decline and Irish Immigration slowed.

Irish Women in New Orleans

Unlike other European emigrants the Irish tended to be unmarried, and many were women. By the close of the 19th Century women outnumbered men (McCaffrey, 2004). Women, often daughters of domestic servants, tended to be better educated than men. Inspired by examples of nuns, they became prominent in teaching and nursing. I see the attitude of women, especially single women, arriving in New Orleans as quite unique. With economic growth solely as their focus it is easy to see once more the influence of Oya/Ezili Danto in the personality of Maman Brigitte as a sustaining force for women to grow and prosper on new soil.

In the decades after the famine more Irish women than men immigrated to the USA. The Irish communities contained more females than males. Irish women differed from most other immigrant women in terms of numbers. In terms of foreign-born women, they outnumbered men. They were the only significant group of women who chose to migrate in primarily female cliques. They accepted jobs most other women turned down, most notably as domestics in wealthy homes (Diner, 1986).

Irish women in America in the last half of the 19th century viewed themselves as self-sufficient beings with economic roles to play in their families and communities in contrast to their American counterparts who led lives of sheltered passivity and enabled domesticity. I feel this is where the empowered female spirit of the Yoruba was embraced by the Irish in the New World. In Louisiana they worked and sent money home. They did this out of family loyalties, as they felt they could better support their families either in or from America rather than in or from Ireland. 'Their actions represented a commitment to Irish Catholic culture and it's way of life' (Diner, 1986). For many women the move across the Atlantic was not made from a longing for a new identity and for a bright new future. Irish women took to the waters to honour the values of the old world to which they were committed. This is, as Diner (1986) says marks the Irish migration experience different to that of Jewish or Italian women. Not only is this an acknowledgement to the old world they had been born into and left but it is also an appreciative nod to their ancestors who had gone before them and sacrificed much for them to have such an opportunity. This is significant in my opinion, as, out of the old, comes the new, is the very crux of Brigid/Brigitte energy.

The Irish famine had a huge impact on the concept of the Irish family and for women. For at least sixty years, young and interestingly, unmarried women left for America in huge numbers. Being unmarried led them to seek employment in different arenas than their married counterparts. Because of such a strong Catholic influence on their upbringing and sexual behaviour Irish women were willing to defer or forgo marriage and family. They sought employment as live-in servants and later as schoolteachers, who were required to remain single. This niche in the labour market was pin pointed by Irish women for Irish women.

The famine left a lasting legacy. The memory of starvation and the inaction of the British became a weapon of national propaganda. Continuous blight on the potato crop lasted for four years. Immigration had begun before the famine and continued well afterwards. The years 1800, 1807, 1816, 1822, and 1839 saw massive crop failures and wide-ranging epidemics that shook rural Ireland to its very bones. By the last decades of the 19th century many young women had no reason to remain in the agricultural towns of Catholic Ireland. They had no realistic chances for marriage or employment. For either to happen, they had to leave the motherland.

Before the famine the poor had large families and married very early in life. The population was huge, even though Immigration was a cultural habit. The humble potato crop fed the large families and was believed to keep the women fertile. Land was divided into smaller and smaller parts so that everyone got a share and could sow a crop of potatoes. (Diner, 1986). After the famine, the practice of having large families declined. The practice of dividing the land stopped. The land of the family was given to one son. Whomever he married, came with a dowry. The dowry was then passed onto one daughter who, in turn, married into another family. The rest of the siblings realised they had to make their own way in the world. The 'unprovided for' girls left to work in Dublin shops, the mills of Lancashire and Manchester, the homes of well-to-do Londoners needing servants or cooks, or they joined the millions of other young Irish women crossing the Atlantic to seek fortune or family already in America. Over time, these became to be seen to be the luckier ones, escaping Ireland for a more comfortable life. Post-Famine family life in Ireland appeared to many as rigid and authoritarian, limiting and circumscribed (Diner, 1986). The family depended on the labour of their children to survive. After the Famine, women's work on the farm changed to poultry and dairy work. By the end of the 19th century wives' work had moved away from the actual functioning of the farm. Work on the farms soon became segregated by gender.

For women, society was as messed up as it can get. Women were inferior to men and were recorded as walking behind their husbands in public as well as feeding their families hot food first and themselves making do with cold scraps or whatever was left over (Diner, 1986). Children were kept in close proximity to parents and ended up doing the parents jobs of raising other siblings. Children raising children. Stifled and frustrated by parental authority they reached for drink or left home. In extreme cases, children withdrew into a delusional world of Schizophrenia. This was possibly born out of the Catholic commandment of honouring thy mother and father and refusing to speak up or stand their ground with their parents. In post-famine Ireland the gender lines became more rigid. Society became extremely divided. Education was segregated, sport was segregated. Rural life was the man's domain where existed all men's social groups and pubs were the place for men to relax after work. This undertone of society told women that they were unwelcome in education with, in the work with and in the social life of men. Where a man works and where he relaxes has no place for women. The disappearance of cottage industries and the capitalisation of butter making in dairies resulted in fewer institutions that brought women together. Pre-Famine Ireland saw women come together to weave in cottage industries and to spin, sing and converse during the whole evening. Now their lives were about work which seemed unending. The social life for women was fitted around the services of the church. Before and after church services women helped each other out and tended to each other in childbirth and sickness (the domain of Brigid).

Women measured their worth on material standards. Both married and unmarried women wanted their own money to support their families (dowries or fare money for their children if married and for their own power if single). For crafts such as knitting, sewing, weaving, lacemaking, women were paid by contractors. Irish women could see no meaningful life for themselves in Ireland. On her own turf, she had no rights, wasn't free, was worked day and night and couldn't develop herself. By the end of the 19th century, Ireland became a place that women left.

Immigration during and after the Famine were the landless and the poor. They were considered excess children by their families. Unwanted and with no resources, there was no other choice. Those that left Irish shores had no intention of returning.

Irish women migrated not as depressed survivors of Famine, but in the main, they made the journey with optimism, in a forward-looking assessment that in America they could achieve a status that they could never have at home (Diner, 1986).

The segregated society that Irish woman left, placed them in a strong position within themselves. Hardened by the man's world in Ireland and their already hunger for economic prosperity propelled them forward to take every opportunity met and make it big in the land of opportunity. Men did not fare so well with emigration. They had come from a society where they were put on a pedestal by the church and their mothers over their female counterparts but in the New World this wasn't the case. The Irish man seemed cursed by the city and the demon drink that frequently took over his life. Men had left a country that had afforded them the greatest respect. Their superior social status was acknowledged by all. For them, moving to the New World was predominantly negative. For women it was positive. The significant status of father was gone after immigration as the whole process of the transfer of land was gone. As his role weakened, the mother's grew. The Irish man yearned for Ireland and their preferential treatment, but the Irish woman didn't. Being Catholic, an Irish husband and wife didn't have the option of divorce as a way of easing marital discord. Many married women, as a result, experienced desertion from their husbands in their new-found homes in New Orleans. If they didn't experience desertion, they lived with chronic alcoholism in their marriage and invariably, through marriage to an older male, they experienced widowhood. Either way, many Irish women found themselves as the sole provider for their families in their new home. On one hand it set the scene for extreme hardship and poverty faced by many Irish women but on the other hand, it enabled and empowered women to grow into the women they could never have been in the countryside back home. This was the influence of Maman Brigitte who, by her very nature, can turn hardship into survival and empowerment.

When Irish women were able to find work as domestics, teachers, nurses and in factories they often opened savings accounts with the local parish priest unbeknownst to their husbands. This general augmentation of female family authority occurred silently (Diner, 1986). And 'silently' also echoes the silent Maman Brigitte. American society placed greater emphasis on carrying out domestic responsibilities such as cooking, cleaning, raising well-disciplined children than had rural Irish society. American popular culture and public opinion held a negative view of the Irish man (Paddy) who was drunken, lazy, unreliable, a poor father figure and brawling. His female equivalent Biddy, on the other hand, even though she was also coarse and drunken was more socially acceptable. Women were viewed as self-sacrificing and doing their best without the aid of their drunken partner. Irish women in comparison to men were civilised and respectable. They wanted middle-class status. They wanted to earn money and respect. Their old Irish ways of being defined by status had followed them on their transoceanic journey.

Single women in America did not favour marriage and those that did, did so, much later in life. Women passed on this tradition to their American-born daughters. Here, on new soil, single Irish women had choices. Their economic motives for migration remained top of their priorities. To marry, meant a sudden loss of their income which was hardship and duress for unskilled workers. This they saw in the crowded tenements of deserted wives or widows.

New World for those that married was problematic- a high rate of domestic violence, frequent desertion of the male breadwinner and a high rate of industrial accidents created many a widow and orphan (Diner, 1986).

In addition to not want to forego their income they were also very loyal to their siblings which was common in the Irish Catholic family dynamic in Ireland. Sending money home for the next brother or sister to come over was ingrained in them and important to them. This was especially common amongst women; women bringing over other women; sisters bringing sisters, aunts bringing their nieces, cousins etc.

Single Irish women sought out domestic service that came with free accommodation. In this sector they faced little competition that they soon dominated. The stereotype of Bridget or Norah carried with it fewer negative implications than did that of Paddy. These women were portrayed as lacking in intelligence, manners, and common sense but at the same time, she was loveable. When Irish women reached America they entered the workforce on the bottom rung, occupying a place equal to that of women of colour. A group with whom they shared many employment experiences. Even though this work was at the very bottom rung, they had left even worse conditions at home in Ireland. Domestic work was a big void nobody wanted to work in, and it was unaffected even during periods of economic downturn. Knowing the privileged position this work had for them they could easily negotiate terms or shop around for the best conditions for them. On American theatre stages they were ridiculed as the 'Biddy the kitchen canary' to which they were indifferent. As a result of the situation that they found themselves in they lived in nice houses and ate leftover good quality food. Many saved impressive sums of money, bought land, sent home money, or bought stained glass windows for their local churches as well as establishing and supporting charitable endeavours. And through all of this she remained a good girl, chaste and uncorrupted by sexual temptation. How she earned her living did not oppose the cultural values or patterns ingrained in her by the church. As a result of her entering domestic service the rate of Irish marriage remained low. Irish girls were fine with being isolated. They had been used to that in Ireland and marriage was not on their agenda. They worked in the company of other servants and got their social fix by participating in church and church related activities. This was important to them. They could refuse a job if the small town had no Irish Catholic community. The most wonderful thing for these women was that by living in a middle-class house they were exposed to the modern world which they couldn't have even imagined in Ireland. The homes of their labour acted as schools to them. In the second half of the 19th century, they wanted to secure their economic lives and took on roles in trade union leadership.

The second wave of Irish women immigrants were mostly found in the teaching profession. The public school system was also unionised by them. Trade unionism needed to improve their earning power if not married. This gives further evidence to the centrality of work in their lives above partnership or marriage. Women who had been deserted, widowed, abused or living with a non-providing husband could not take advantage of the opportunities afforded by America unlike their single sisters. The lives of poverty which was their experience in the overcrowded slums highlighted the differences between being married and remaining single. Women turned to alcohol and petty crime but very rarely to prostitution. The Irish came to the USA poorer than other immigrants at that time. Mental illness caused by poverty, abandonment, widowhood, and horrible marriages was the experience for these women. Irish society stressed fighting, aggressiveness, and combativeness. Women fought with the men and with other women and in public much to the disgust of American women. Maman Brigitte in New Orleans is often said to be foul-mouthed and a lover of rum. I wonder if the loud, brawling Irish had anything to do with that particular side of Brigitte.

Irish Women and Haitian Women's
Common Experience in New Orleans

Both Irish and Haitian women shared many commonalities, it seems, when they arrived in large numbers in New Orleans. It is not unusual for people to turn to their faith when in times of stress. Faith, whether it is to the divine or to the spirits act as a comfort and role models to the believers. The Irish women brought their Catholic faith with them, in particular the Virgin Mother Mary and Saint Brigid. The Virgin Mary was to the Irish, the all-encompassing Great Mother who had an impossible standard to live up to. However, with Mary in their hearts, Irish women rarely ever turned to prostitution even when times were extremely bad. Times became very bad for women when their men deserted them or died, leaving them alone to fend for themselves and their families.

As discussed in the previous chapters Irish women led fairly miserable lives in the shadow of male supremacy in their Irish homeland. This was similar for Haitian women who also lived within a misogynistic patriarchal culture. Brown (2010) narrates how Haitians struggled to adapt both during and after slavery but in the case of women, they seemed to gain social and economic power when they shifted from rural to urban life, much like the women from Ireland. Similar to Irish family life, Haitian family life, which was the main domain of women became smaller in the New World. Both groups of women found their voices and fostered a proactive attitude which enabled them to advance economically. In comparison their male counterparts did not cope very well once the land was removed from the picture. Like Irish men, Haitian men were raised to exert power and authority but in their new city surroundings they had no means to do this. Where the women loudly voiced their wares for sale at markets, the men slumped into the background muttering into the drink or turning to gambling. Women from Ireland and Haiti, unfettered by an agri-focal society propelled themselves forward without male assistance.

Returning once more to how Maman Brigitte is sometimes portrayed with tape over her mouth, I question why this is so, now that she is in the New World where anything is possible. In ceremony in New Orleans:

...though whites and free colored police were known to have spied on ceremonies, an oath, sometimes sealed with goat's blood, bound all participants to secrecy on pain of death (Geggus, 1991).

Was her silence hand in hand with her secrecy, with her power? Has her silence been intentional on her own behalf, on society's behalf or is it to correspond with the silence of her domain, the graveyard? If the latter were the case, then the mouth of Baron Samedi would also be taped, and this is not the case. Was she so distressed in her new country that she simply stopped talking that echoes the condition of pa-pale? Was her taped mouth a nod to the old world where female voices were not only not encouraged but frowned upon? Maman Brigitte is said to be foul mouthed as is Baron Samedi, her husband so, did society have a problem with the little lady's potty mouth and intentionally shut her up to give more air space to her husband? Starhawk (2011) speaks of silence thusly:

Silence can be a mark of oppression or a source of strength. We must learn to contain our power and when to express it, how to offer service to the great powers of life and death and to our communities without falling into servitude

This could mean her silence is a containment of her power before she lets rip, like the afore-mentioned great Kali-Ma. Her silence could be viewed as a stark warning of what is to come, like the calm before the storm.

When the hearts of Haitian and Irish women came together in the New World for a new empowered life, their needs and wants helped birth a new version of who and what was dear to them from their cultures. With deliberate intention together they birthed Maman Brigitte. The best of both worlds. Her brashness and sex loving qualities surpassed the Catholic restrictions imposed on women in Irish culture whilst her youthful appearance facilitated the rebirth of Gran Brijit with all her wisdom from Haitian culture in their new territory, they now called home. This was done with an awareness of their origins in the African homeland, where we have all originated and where women were tribal and cult leaders. It is possible that her silenced mouth represents the old world for both Haitians and Irish, particularly Haitian and Irish women.

Maybe this was the case for Maman Brigitte. The needs of women were different in New Orleans than they were in their repressed homelands. They needed a figure who would motivate, empower, and sustain them as they embraced their new world of opportunity and independence, only dreamed of before. New Orleans was a new society that brought both black and white together. Here, as the city greeted the two more similar than dissimilar cultures, it cradled the similar and the diverse in her swampy waters before birthing a new spirit that possessed the old world in her shadow and silence but who was ready for the New World and all that it would bring to the brave seeker.

Maman Brigitte in New Orleans
When writing this book, I knew I couldn't bring this book to life if I didn't travel to either Haiti or Louisiana. For the months that I spent researching and writing I toyed with both destinations and in the end, I decided on Louisiana. The reason was twofold. Firstly, at the time of writing, Haiti was not recommended as a tourist destination due to civil unrest and violence which

was unfortunate. Seeing as Haiti was where Vodou began and where Brigitte was birthed, I was hoping to connect to that space. Another time, hopefully. Secondly, I had researched so much about my Irish ancestors travelling to America, I felt like I wanted to walk in their footsteps and almost pretend I too was arriving to the New World. Truth be told, I always had an interest in the Deep South and I was super excited about finally going.

I arrived in New Orleans late in the evening in August 2023. I was excited but unsure what to expect. I wasn't prepared for the intense heat of the Deep South which enveloped me as soon as I stepped outside the airport. For this trip I had arranged to meet with a dear friend. I don't usually travel with company, so it was nice to share this experience with somebody else. Ann was eager to experience the jazz scene. I was eager to experience the Voodoo scene and to discover what I could about Maman Brigitte. I felt I had gleaned what I could from research, I really just wanted some local knowledge and to feel the energy of the city. This city that is called the Crescent City and is considered 'the most feminine of women' (McKinney, 2006). I wanted to feel the dark feminine energy of Brigitte and view the curved Mississippi river that rebirthed and redefined her right there in the Crescent City.

Once I made the decision to travel to New Orleans, I knew that I would encounter someone there who could share something personally about Maman Brigitte or indeed point me in the direction of further research. For the first couple of days, I had booked a cemetery tour and a Voodoo walking tour to get started. I wasn't blown away by either of them but on one of the tours an authentic Voodoo shop was casually dropped into conversation which resonated with me. Once the tour ended and we had eaten we headed in the direction of *Voodoo Authentica*. I immediately liked the energy of the shop. As the name suggested, it certainly seemed to be the real deal. Before long, from the back room emerged a modern Haitian Voodoo Priestess by the name of Cate with a big smile on her face. I began firing question after question at her, which she answered but I was retaining none of the information with my excitement. I eventually calmed down and explained why I was so eager to hear her answers. Cate kindly agreed to an interview with me in a week's time. I was bursting with excitement. This was the reason I had travelled to New Orleans, to meet a genuine Haitian priestess who could give first hand, personal information about her Voodoo practice and share some information about how she understands Maman Brigitte and this was why I had been guided to go to New Orleans. This is for me, further proof of how magically and synchronously the goddess works.

Speaking to Cate about my love for Brigid and her love for her path was an emotional experience. From Priestess to Priestess, we chatted about our heritage and spiritual direction. Cate asked many questions about Brigid and I asked her about her Voodoo path and who Brigitte is for her. The entire interview is too long to transcribe for this book but I include two short snippets on who the Gede nation are for Cate and also how she understands Brigitte.

Cate: 'I call the Gede the funky bunch. They are so fun and energetic. They constantly tell dick jokes. Constantly! Even if you don't speak Creole, it doesn't matter. They'll let you know what the punch line is. They'll interrupt other parts of the ceremony. When you're serving a gentle, clean spirit all of a sudden one of them will pop up in possession.

But when Brigitte and Baron appear that energy is different even though they are Gede. When they appear, there is a more sombre and frightening tone. I think the Gede serve to remind us of all the fun stuff we can do when we have a physical body like; drinking, dancing, having sex. Brigitte and Baron bring a sober reminder that we all should be having a good time and loving ourselves and being present in our bodies, but we also need to remember, like right in your face, literally on the ground in front of you that there is a bigger picture to that reverence'.

When I asked her how she understands Brigitte, she replied:

Cate: 'Maman Brigitte is the mother of the cemetery. She is the counterpart to Papa Gede as Gran Brijit and counterpart to Baron Samedi as Maman Brigitte. A lot of folks look at Brigitte with both fear and reverence but also with a maternal connection. It's a very complicated dynamic with her.'

Cate: 'Brigitte is maternal sure, but she is somebody who is feared by a lot of people who get away with stuff in their lives, like terrible things that they don't account for. These people might even be able to slip under the radar when they pass with left-handed spirits of the dead. Maman Brigitte is the one who will put her foot down on that person. Not even in the afterlife are you going to be prancing around causing harm to people. It's like fuck you. There is a side of her that is very much seen as a persecutor of forgotten criminals that were never brought to justice. Not in the sense of stealing a loaf of bread and you never got caught, not like that. People who like, harm children, and get away with it. The law doesn't do anything about it. They think they'll pass away in their sleep, and all is good. But no! There she is!

She's also associated with the screech owl which is one of the most terrifying animals in the night. The screech owl is also associated with violent spirits. So, she really does have that side to her that is feared, not as a doer of evil but as someone who will not let you away with it'.

Pauline: 'Fascinating because in Ireland, Brigid is credited with introducing the whistle to help protect women from rape and violence. The whistle too is such a shrill noise'.

Cate: 'Maman Brigitte is connected to that too! With women and children and especially with pregnant women, all mothers, young and old who are being sexually victimised. She is absolutely associated with these women and seen as a protector of them'.

Standing at the Mississippi I couldn't help but feel a sense of both sadness and happiness for the fate of many Irish women arriving in Louisiana for a new life. I was standing where these women took their first steps to freedom and empowerment. In New Orleans they would step off the ship and hopefully become the best version of themselves in the land of opportunity. And if this wasn't to be their experience, they would continue to blend with the other outcast in society, people of colour. Regardless, their experience in the New World would be watched over by Maman Brigitte who would notice everything and either provide comfort through her spiritual presence in this city or be a beacon of brighter days to come.

The American south, too, was a place where the perceived status of the Irish was deeply entwined with, and inextricably related, to, that of blacks (Giemza, 2012).

This is presumably where the colours green and black come from that are largely associated with Brigitte. We saw previously how the experience of Haitian and Irish women were not so dissimilar. Many mothers and wives shared the same fate of abandonment or widowhood in the New World. Both cultures came from cultures of female inferiority and suddenly found space in New Orleans to work, barter and compete in the markets to sell their wares. Both races were also fond of religious veneration. 'Wailing notes' of Irish mourners during the famine of 1845–1846 were said to be similar of slave songs (Giemza, 2012). With Oya in Haitian hearts and Brigid in Irish hearts and possibly too in Haitian hearts it is possible that these fiery deities kept the home fires burning in their new land. And within those fires was a new Lwa for all women on Louisianan ground that connected the old world to the new in the form of Brigitte.

I had hoped to see art of her in various Voodoo shops and I had hoped to hear her being mentioned locally, but apart from the interview with Cate that wasn't so. I saw a huge painting of the Baron by a local artist in a shop. When I enquired if there was a similar painting for Brigitte the answer was 'no'. I found that when I asked about Brigitte with local guides, they said they had heard of her but after that they knew very little. They all had heard of the Baron though! I was disappointed to say the least but maybe this is why I am writing this book. Maybe there really isn't much available on her and now is her time to emerge as the dark goddess that she is, from out of her counterpart's shadow and into the forefront. By shining a spotlight on her and all that she can assist with, maybe in time, we can include Brigitte into the list of dark goddesses and give her credit where credit is due.

Chapter 3

Maman Brigitte in Today's World

Maman Brigitte

Maman Brigitte is an Afro-Irish dark Goddess. She, along with her counterpart the Baron, rule over everything we fear, most notably death. Maman Brigitte resides in the underworld and within each of us in our shadow. When I consider Maman Brigitte, I feel the term *Maîtresse* (Mistress) captures her essence the most. As *Maîtresse* she is seductive, enigmatic, mysterious, aromatic, sensual and vibrant. She has a large presence if not fierce. There is no better nor fiercer presence to call upon when in despair. She will not magic away your suffering or pain. She will sit with you and hold space as you journey down into that pain. Only then, can you recognise your own strength and begin the transformative process from pain and suffering to empowerment and healing. Maman Brigitte embodies the grand total of female history and can be invoked to aid with all of the following:

Abandonment

I already wrote about how many women experienced abandonment in the New World by their partners or spouses. Abandonment had already existed in the old world before setting sail for better conditions. Women have been abandoned by many religious organisations as being mostly unequal and unwelcome in roles of authority within the church specifically reserved for men. Society as a result has abandoned women as being equal citizens. Nowhere has this been more evident in the barbaric treatment of unmarried mothers as opposed to unmarried fathers by the Catholic church, most notably in Ireland. This atrocity continues as children were torn from their mothers and brought up as abandoned children of the state. The pain of this continues down through family lineages and will need much healing after stifled anger and rage has been expressed. Call upon Brigitte to sit with you as you express the hurt of abandonment.

Ancestral Healing

Brigitte emerged in the Caribbean and the Americas when enforced slavery was in operation and when it was abolished. Within each eventually freed person of colour was the cellular memory of enslavement, hardship and trauma. From the Irish diaspora cellular memory of colonization, famine and repression ran through the blood and veins of all new immigrants. Within each of us today are memories both good and bad of the generations gone before us. The witch wound is also within many of us, when we were shamed, beaten and killed for being different. Call upon Brigitte to sit with you as you acknowledge the pain of your ancestors and honour them by either consciously breaking the lineage of pain and seeking healing.

Death

Death is the ultimate darkness that we all fear. This fear has kept us gripping onto life, fearing ageing, fearing the repercussions of our sinful behaviour, fearing the void and dreading the silence. Maman Brigitte showed the Irish in the New World that there is another perspective. One where the dead and the living can co-exist, even if the Otherworld is invisible. The Otherworld was once a major tenet of indigenous Irish Celtic belief. Death was not sensed with trepidation but seen as a reprieve from the challenges of this life. Life was a circular concept that began and ended in darkness. The concept of death changed with the slow introduction of Christianity in Ireland. Gradually, time became linear with start and end points. Birth was the start and death loomed as the terrifying end. Maman Brigitte is the gatherer of lost souls in the Otherworld. She is the Dark Mother energy that is available to everyone, especially to the downtrodden and outcasts in society Her territory is the graveyard which is the realm of the dead but yet exists in the living world. She can flit between both, inhabit both, belong to both and yet belong to neither. To the living, she is brave, strong, wise, a portal to lost loved ones and a bridge that will unite them to their loved ones when their time comes. To the dead, she is their vessel to commune with the living and she is the ultimate Mother to the otherwise forgotten in death. She is also the guardian of their graves, protecting the dead from black magic. As a Lwa of both life and death she is eternal. Maman Brigitte brings endless possibilities in death. Death is merely another passage into a new existence. Call upon Brigitte for all matters linked to death, death of loved ones, death of a relationship, death of a way of living and fear of death.

Detachment

To be able to detach is a wonderful way of observing what is going on around you without being immersed in a flood of emotions. Our family dynamic or our painful patterns sometimes require us to step back and look at the situation through a more detached perspective. Here we can see unhealthy patterns that continue to play out, producing the same unfulfilling outcomes. Here we can also see our choices and how they impact on our day to day lives. Much like Irish women who set sail for New Orleans they left with an air of detachment. They knew they most probably would never return. Instead of looking through rose-tinted glasses they were able to see the culture they were leaving for what it was at that time – no friend to women, particularly to single women. Call upon Brigitte to sit with you as you remove yourself from the drama to see the bigger picture and see things in their true perspective.

Displacement

As a result of large families with only a dowry for one daughter, I have written about how many Irish daughters were pushed out to fend for themselves. They were either forced to move to larger cities or to emigrate. With the Famine of 1845 many Irish women took the boat to America. Although it was a rebirthing and a new beginning of good fortune never imagined in Ireland, it was forced because of the failed potato crop rather than a choice. If these women never felt good enough to have been given a dowry or if they had had their youths spent on raising their mother's children, they must have felt extremely vulnerable leaving home without a strong sense of belonging or even of having been validated as a person. For African women being forcibly removed from their homesteads where they knew all herbs, plants and animal kingdom they must have been at odds with themselves in their new surroundings. Haitian women that moved to New Orleans and beyond after the Haitian revolution would have experienced the same upheaval. Call upon Brigitte to lament the old country and sit with you while you re-root yourself into a new time and space.

Fear

Fear wears many coats; Fear of the unknown, fear of the known, fear of violence against women, fear of failure; economic and personal, fear of the living, fear of the dead, fear of your limitations, fear of your potential. Call upon Brigitte to clarify what fear needs to be faced within you.

Finding Your Voice

Showing up, speaking up and standing up for yourself. Speaking about your problems is acknowledging them and validating your feelings. By unmuting yourself you begin your metamorphosis into your highest potential. The good catholic girl was quiet and demure and knew her place within Irish society. Saint Brigid was also quiet and demure, but the Goddess Brigid didn't know her place. She transcended all territory unlike other Goddesses who were equated with specific regions in Ireland. By transcending not only the whole isle of Erin, Brigid morphed into Maman Brigitte that took pleasure in and expressed her sexuality, away from the Catholic church. Call upon Brigitte to scream your anger, to call it out when you see it, to voice your needs to yourself firstly then to others in your life.

Gratitude

There is always something to be grateful for. Even amidst the entanglement of overwhelm and pain there is always someone, something or some situation that is a blessing in your life. If you cannot name someone or something, then maybe you yourself are the positive and you need to go find a similar tribe of enriching souls. Maybe you can't see one or two blessings in your life because of how much you are hurting. Even in the darkest days of enslavement there was dancing and community gatherings at night on the camps in Haiti and also in Congo square in New Orleans. If you cannot see the light, ask Brigitte to sit with you in the dark until you perceive the light.

Grief

After every death comes grief. In our history grief came with emigration, displacement, enslavement, abandonment and struggling to survive. Grief for the abandoned islands of Haiti and Eire. Grief was in the hearts of siblings and family members left behind knowing that the family dynamic had changed forever. Call upon Brigitte to lament and express your grief after any type of death.

Homelessness

Homelessness or the fear of homelessness makes us feel vulnerable and unsafe. Many Irish people experienced eviction as a result of colonialisation and this fear was also in the immigrants who crossed the Atlantic for a fresh start. Some found wonderful homes, others did not. At a time of massive numbers of homelessness in contemporary Ireland that fear has returned for too many people. Call upon Brigitte to express this fear.

Loss

We experience loss each and every day as we continue to grow and change, moving out of our tiny cocoons either created by ourselves or by the expectations of others. As we continue to grow, we can feel out of our depth even if it is ultimately what we crave. Life itself is loss and death, as it feels to our aching hearts is the ultimate experience of loss. Even if the relationship, job, partnership or location is toxic, it can still feel like a loss when we move on. Call upon Brigitte to sit with you as you express loss and to help you process previous losses that went unacknowledged.

Loss of Self

Many women lose themselves in partnerships or in motherhood. These women lead lives in service to their families at the expense of honouring other aspects of themselves. With the passage of time, they feel they are unrecognisable to themselves and lost. In abusive situations the once chased wild spirit becomes something that must be repressed and controlled. Call upon Brigitte to show you your strength to remove labels and images that are not yours or that you have outgrown or never liked. Call upon Brigitte to express your rage or sorrow at having allowed others to repress you and to gather up lost parts of yourself.

Maternal Issues

The Great Mother on both sides of the world. For us here in Ireland she is the Great Mother Goddess in life. In New Orleans and Haiti, she is the Great Mother Goddess in death. Life giver and life taker. For all mother issues that include loss of a mother, rejection by a mother, ignored by a mother, removed from a mother, call upon Brigitte to sit with you as you acknowledge your mother wound. Within each of us we carry the effects of the collective mother wound where the sacred feminine has been repressed and vilified. Call upon Brigitte to remember Her and reconnect to Her.

Overshadowing

Overshadowing for many Irish women before the Famine in Ireland included being pushed into the background of the family if there was no dowry for marriage or if marriage wasn't their choice. It also included being pushed to the forefront to step up to mothering their siblings as was often the case in common large families in Ireland. Children rearing children. Nobody's needs were met save having a full belly and a roof over their heads. In marriage Irish women were often overshadowed by their husbands and marriages were often out of financial rather than loving reasons. This misogynistic culture of male supremacy was also the experience of the Haitian woman. Call upon Brigitte to remember your worth and reclaim your sovereignty.

Persecution

For all matters of justice call upon Brigitte and her strong presence to step out and shine a light on all perpetrators of evil. For any injustice that has happened to you or a loved one or what you have felt in the world, call upon Brigitte.

Protection

Brigitte is protector of all lost souls wandering in between worlds with nobody waiting for them in the next life. She gathers them all and welcomes into the family Gede. She keeps them with her and protects their graves. She is the protector of women and children and all the vulnerable in society. For any issues with which you need protection call upon Brigitte to toughen you up, stand your ground or call it out.

Shadow Work

Our shadow is not just where all our 'bad' parts of ourselves lurk. Within our shadows lie our potential, forgotten or repressed aspects of ourselves or what we fear. The shadow is an integral part to our whole self. We can never be whole if we deny or suppress this part of us. We never need to deep dive in and become overwhelmed especially if we have intentionally placed huge traumas here. But what we can do, is understand that we have a shadow. The shadow resides in ourselves and every other person. If we can acknowledge our shadow, we might identify what is in need of healing. Call upon Brigitte to identify your shadow aspect that wants attention and ask her to steer you towards the best course of action to begin your healing journey.

Slave to Routine

All work and no play does not need to be our modern experience. Although we can claim to be slaves to the routine or to the job, we are not. Unlike our African ancestors and indentured servants, we have freedom and choices. If we are working too much and not enjoying earthly pleasures Brigitte can help you remember what fun life can be. Call upon Brigitte to help you loosen up and have fun.

Strength

Having a strong back bone to push yourself forward and stand your ground takes time to cultivate. If we push ourselves out of our comfort zones too quickly, we will crumble like a deck of cards. However, we need to remember we are a constant work in progress, and we need to continuously move forward, even at a gentle but consistent pace. Call upon Brigitte to find the strength to say 'yes' to opportunities that help you grow even if saying yes feels overwhelming.

Survival

Irish and Haitian women were made of strong stuff and could for the most part vocalise their financial needs. Between them their voices were heard shouting their wares for sale at markets, negotiating better conditions as domestic servants or asking for work in factories. In any matter of survival call upon Brigitte to support and guide you up out of despair.

Thriving

Thriving was the ability of immigrants to come together in their communities and unite in power. Within a couple of generations these women would evolve out of the working class and into the middle class positions of teachers, nurses, journalists etc. They would have the financial means to strengthen their communities through their churches and they would be able to save their siblings by bring them over to the New World. Call upon Brigitte to celebrate your successes no matter how small and to keep you moving forward and thriving.

Colours Associated with Maman Brigitte

Black

Black, the most synonymous colour of death. Black is the darkest colour, the opposite of light. For this reason, it has been very much used in description to convey inferiority and malevolence, especially within Christian doctrine. Black is almost the ultimate threat to the pure light of God. Black is, however, a colour of mystery and enigma. When I conjure up the colour black in my mind I am reminded of the magician's magical cloak, beneath which all magic happens. The magician can use the cloak to reveal hidden items or indeed use it to cloak himself in invisibility and disappear with a sudden whoosh. I am also reminded of the powerful forge attributed to Brigid. Within her deep, dark forge all creative acts of transformation occur. Within her dark forge lies infinite potential. Black is a very powerful colour representing the void of life that provides for the germination of seed. In the midst of this absence of life all life emerges. It is associated with the deep earth, the dark cave and, of course, a dark cemetery. Black also death, grief and mourning as well as emitting a frequency of power, elegance, sophistication, prestige, and authority. As guardian of the cemetery, it is little wonder that black and all its deathly connotations are one of Brigitte's colours.

Green

Brigitte, like Brigid of Ireland, is associated with mothering and healing. It is no surprise that the colour green is ascribed to both variants of her. Mostly, associated with the colour of Ireland's green fields the colour could represent the isle of Eire in general that formed part of Brigitte's identity. Green is, of course, connected to the heart chakra and its capability to love and protect. It is the colour of growth, renewal, abundance, health and hope. Green is a colour to stimulate communication, intelligence, adaptability and clear thinking. As it is a dominant colour of nature, it is the colour to symbolise new beginnings after death which is ultimately what death itself represents, new beginnings.

Red

Red, the colour of life itself, of blood and menstruation goes hand in hand with the energy of Brigitte. As lady of the Gede she oozes life-affirming qualities linked to sexuality and passion. Brigitte is often depicted with flaming red hair like her Irish counterpart. She is also representative of fire and it's cleansing but also deadly properties. Brigid of Ireland was also connected to the colour red which was the colour of the Otherworld and her cow was said to have been red-eared which demonstrated its otherworldly origins. Red is the colour of courage, warmth, joy, leadership, excitement, determination, drive and survival. All of these attributes can be related to Brigitte.

Purple
Purple is the colour of wisdom, luxury, pride, extravagance, dignity, spirituality. Bravery and confidence. I see these traits very much correlated to the Benin Goddess, Oya, who features in the blended personality of Brigitte. The colour purple is connected to the crown chakra which is the chakra closest to the divine and to the higher self.

Animals Associated with Maman Brigitte

The Screech Owl
The screech owl is representative of the underworld and is an omen of death. It is a relayer of truth. It has the ability to penetrate the darkness and is therefore associated with wisdom and intuition. The Crone or the Cailleach is likened to the season of winter and death and is often associated with the owl. It is said that she can morph into an owl at will. Brigitte, although being younger than the Cailleach, possesses many of her abilities and contains much of her wisdom. Her essence as Gran Brijit can be equated with the Crone/Cailleach.

The Black Rooster
The Black rooster is traditionally symbolic of power, victory and asserting one's authority. The dark feathers can also be viewed as protective of the flock, warding off predators and

evil. This is most befitting of the characteristics of Brigitte who is considered protectress of the dead, their graves and protectress of the living, especially women and children. The protective symbolism of the black rooster extends to t malevolent spirits which are said to lurk at the cemetery looking to turn corpses into zombies. Again, it is no surprise that the black rooster is affiliated with the shielding energies of Brigitte. The crawing sound made by the rooster is said to alert evil and even be the sound of imminent good luck. It is also representative of the sun and dawn which could be indicative of the rebirth brought about by death. It may be suggestive too of hope and of an improvement in the conditions of life. Another trail of thought could be that the rooster is the cock which links into the sexual expression, abandonment and freedom of Brigitte.

The Spider
The spider scurrying out from under a hard rock comes to mind when I think of spiders and the cemetery. The spider is another symbol of new beginnings and cycles. With her eight legs she is quite the manifester and weaver of her reality. The spider woman features in Native American mythology as the creatrix of life on earth. With her intricate skill and detail, she wove the world into being and is the spinner and weaver of destiny. The spider is a mother figure and teaches perseverance, diligence, and patience. As Mother Goddess She is also representative of survival which is one of Brigitte's most associated traits.

Symbols Associated with Maman Brigitte

The Coffin
The coffin is one of the main symbols of death. It is a form of protection for the deceased body ensuring that no harm will

come to the body from scavengers or from grave robbers. Brigitte and the Baron watch over all graves.

The Cemetery

The cemetery is the one of the most peaceful places on earth. Not only does it serve as a place for the living to visit their dead, but it also is a place to mediate and contemplate one's own mortality. Cemeteries are a stark reminder of what is coming down the road for each and every one of us. Brigitte is the female guardian at each cemetery.

The Cross

The cross is placed at a crossroads in the cemetery to demonstrate the crossing of the earthly and the spiritual worlds. Brigitte is the traveller between the worlds and is the meeter and greeter for all new souls in death.

Skulls

The skull is a symbol of death and mortality. It is a symbol of gratitude toward life. Brigitte and the Baron know how to celebrate life whilst also keeping a serious outlook on life.

The Voodoo Hat

The top hat is more associated with the Baron than Brigitte. It is a powerful symbol of gentlemanliness and status. It is sometimes linked with Brigitte. As it covers the head it is said to contain thought. This to me represents her intellectual capabilities and her connection to the higher realm or the upper world where life beyond this world exists.

Days Associated with Maman Brigitte

Days pertinent to Brigitte are Fridays and Saturdays. Fridays and Saturdays are typically associated with letting your hair down and having fun.

Offerings to Maman Brigitte

Offerings to Maman Brigitte include rum, hot peppers, dark chocolate, and cigars. She is a fun time Lwa, after all, that enjoys the simple pleasures of life.

Connecting to Maman Brigitte

Every appearance of Brigid has a season, a most perfect time in the natural cycle of life to connect deeply to her. Brigitte is no exception. Although you can connect to her at any time and what she represents for you, Samhain is a perfect time to really feel this energy. Samhain is a natural time of death and decay as we approach the wintertime of stillness. Samhain and its similar energies are celebrated in Haiti as Fet Gede also around this time. Samhain and Fet Gede remind us to take stock of the role our ancestors played and all those who came before us.

As the darkness starts to dominate in our worlds we can step into that energy and see where we are in need of healing at this time. Although the emotions associated with the darkness are heavy and somewhat frightening, know that like the season, they cannot hold their strength forever. Everything has a season. And once you work with Brigitte, the dark goddess, she will have your back.

You can connect to Brigitte with your intention. Maybe you can source a picture of her, or you can illustrate how she feels to you if you are creative. If that is not your thing you can simply just get a sense of the dark goddess and the richness she can bring to your life through her wisdom through any natural or material object that illustrates her energy or vibe.

Meditate on what you would like help with at this time and whatever comes to mind, that's what is in need of healing. Remember she is mostly attributed to issues of abandonment, ancestral healing, death, displacement, fear, finding your voice, gratitude for life, grief, loss, loss of self, maternal issues, persecution, protection, seeing the bigger picture, shadow work, slave to the routine, strength; emotional and physical, survival, thriving and any other issue that is relevant to you. Allow one of these to make itself known to you.

Wear one or all of her colours and understand consciously why you are drawn to or choosing the colour(s) that you have chosen. By wearing one or more of her colours connected to her at this time you are opening yourself up to their and her qualities.

You can write your own invocation to her or you can use this one below that I wrote.

A sample invocation to Brigitte:
Maman Brigitte
Maman Brigitte
Maman Brigitte
I call thee thrice,
Great lady of the dark,
Queen of the night,
Present,
When the owl doth screech.

Create an altar for her with simple offerings as mentioned earlier. On your altar add an image of her along with other items associated with her such as an owl, dirt from a cemetery or a picture of an ancestor. To connect to her energy, you could draw her veve on black paper and maybe commit to a 13-day practice of consciously connecting with her each day. I always feel that 13 is a powerful number linked to the sacred feminine.

A sample prayer to Brigitte
Hail Brigitte full of wisdom,
Great guardian of graves,
Blessed are you amongst the forgotten and abandoned.
Blessed is your deathly realm of earth and bones,

Surrounded and enclosed by your Oak.
Oh mighty mistress,
Passionate protectress,
Dweller of the dark,
Hear my call, Lady of the night,
Ease my pain and show me my way,
Guide, strengthen and protect me,
Today and all of my tomorrows.
So mote it be,
Dark Goddess Brigitte.

Conclusion

Who is Brigitte? For me, she is authenticity, that stirring in the subconscious that arouses the conscious mind's attention to our buried pain that needs healing for us to be who we are meant to be. She is the silent nudge, to wake up and notice what is false and unserving in our lives. Facing the unknown road and dealing with all our fears requires courage. When we think we can't do it, Brigitte is the force that reminds us that we can. She draws attention to the hardships endured by the human family during the slave trade and for me, by my Irish ancestors who emigrated to the Americas. She shows us that survival is possible. And like the lotus in mud, she reminds us that within our pain, not only can we survive but we can thrive. Brigitte loves to laugh and have fun but mirrors accountability for all the decisions we make in life. She teaches us that death is inevitable for us all and in both life and death she is present as the dark mother goddess.

What has Brigitte taught me? To be authentic you need to take responsibility for your issues and do deep soul work. You cannot step into your power if you are shunning your shadow. Dealing with your issues is a way of becoming whole again and this is a constant work in progress. The very heavy emotions may lift but we have many layers to work through. We must acknowledge this within ourselves and within each other. When it is time to take the deep dive, she is there to lead and bear witness, if you embrace her.

As the dark goddess she shows us that to be authentic we must bridge the parts of us that we lost or ignored back from the subconscious into our consciousness. On this journey, we will discard instead of gain. We will see the obvious advantage of allowing scenarios and situations to die in our lives. We will drop labels or associations which were never ours in the beginning or which have served their purpose. The more we do this, the more authentic we become.

Brigitte has made me very much aware of my timely existence on earth. The clock ticks each day for us all. We have all come forth into life for a specific reason. Understanding this has enabled me to see clearly what is important to me and to try to do my best to achieve my life's purpose. Viewing my life's mission from this understanding has made the passing of other souls easier for me as I understand their death to be a completion of their life's *raison d'être.*

Brigitte has reminded me once more that she is a face of the goddess. Acknowledging her as Great Mother Goddess has allowed me to feel safe to dive deep down into the familial, ancestral and cultural mother wounds. I connected to Brigid as Mother Goddess when I dedicated to her as Daughter of Brigid. Once I dedicated as her Priestess, I knew I needed to travel deeper into my subconscious and heal further if I was to become a stronger version of myself. The essential component of stepping up into my power and moving forward required a part of me to die. That part was the stuck part of my inner child. The part that still operated on past conditioning and wounding. If part of my inner child needed to die, then the remaining part would need a rebirthing. I needed a strong, powerful energy to push me through this. And this energy was Maman Brigitte. In her lore, she died several times in order to be rebirthed.

Maman Brigitte prompts me to loosen up and have fun. Life is short. She calls for straight talking: to say it straight, call a spade a spade. And to stop being a slave to work! There is more to life. When you work with Brigitte you take a solemn dive into your subconscious, and new times will inevitably be born for you if you do the necessary work. Before the new dawn, the descent into the darkness must happen. The dark precedes the light. The way it is in the natural world.

The energy of Maman Brigitte is different to Brigid. They are different faces of the same coin. Goddess is one side of the coin, but the sides of goddess and saint are different as are the sides of goddess/saint and Voodoo deity. For me Maman Brigitte has a more forceful façade and energy than Brigid. As dark goddess she is the tough mother rather than the soft, comforting mother. She reveals herself as someone who is powerful and who will turn you into a much stronger version of yourself if you feel her nudge. She is a take it or leave it energy. You know where I am, when you're ready. If you're not ready now, come back when you are. There is no cajoling. You are either ready to let some part of you die or you're not. When you come before her, she points the way, but you are free and alone as you travel into the shadows. She doesn't accompany you. Why should she? She did her journey alone. She overshadows your path, but you are alone. Her laughter in the depths of the shadow remind you of the transforming soul work you are undertaking which will birth a new world experience for you if you are brave enough.

Feeling my way into her energy I am not met by an old crone archetype. She is younger than the crone, not young like the maiden or lover but she is not ancient. She has acquired the mysteries and the wisdom of life from a hard life, and she takes pleasure in the moment where she can from sex, rum and having a good laugh. Her experience has included isolation, abandonment, survival, poverty, rejection and death. She has come out the other end. Holding no bitterness, she still loves life and all the available earthly pleasures that are available to us. She encompasses the *femme forte* (strong woman) spirit. She has been there, done that and not only bought the t-shirt but built the factory.

Maman Brigitte is the primal mother. She is a fiercely defending energy that keeps her eye on you but waits for you to make up your own mind to journey into the darkness. It is with this acknowledgement that I can now understand why she is mostly depicted as silent. Lilith Dorsey concludes her book *Orishas, Goddesses and Voodoo Queens* very beautifully when she writes:

> *Maman Brigitte, my mother, who helps me find truth and justice on even the darkest of nights. Your silence means there are no words but only the most powerful love* (Dorsey, 2020).

And there it is. Her silence is love. Within the silent cemetery in the dark of the night, her silence cradles the spirit world. Her silent presence over the Otherworld is rarely spoken about in the land of the living but we all have a deep knowing that our ancestors are safe on the other side of life. Through the darkness she wanders through the worlds, safeguards those resting and yet keeps an eye out for new arrivals to welcome them home. Great lady of the dark, protectress of our unseen, it is time to break *our* silence and speak your name, Maman Brigitte our loving mother and dark goddess of Africa and Ireland.

Bibliography

Avery, Mick., 2005. The Spirit Within. Spirit Teaching © Ltd.

Bascom, W.R., 1992. *African folktales in the New World.* Bloomington: Indiana University Press.

Birnbaum, L.C., *Dark Mother: African Origins and Godmothers,* iUniverse.com, (2001).

Brown, K.M., 2010. *Mama Lola: A Vodou priestess in Brooklyn* (Vol. 4). Univ of California Press.

Catháin, S.Ó., 1995. *The Festival of Brigit: Celtic Goddess and Holy Woman.* DBA.

Condren, M., 1989. *The Serpent and the Goddess: Women, Religion, and Power in Celtic Ireland,* Harper & Row.

Cosentino, D.J., 1995. *Sacred arts of Haitian Vodou.* [publisher not identified].

Davis, W., 2010. *The serpent and the rainbow.* Simon and Schuster.

De Courcy, J., 1986. *Ireland and the Irish in maritime history.* Dublin, Ireland: Glendale Press.

Denzer, LaRay., "Yoruba Women: A Historiographical Study." *The International Journal of African Historical Studies,* vol. 27, no. 1, 1994, pp. 1–39. JSTOR, https://doi.org/10.2307/220968. Accessed 23 July 2023.

Deren, M., 1970. Divine Horsemen: The Living Gods of Haiti. 1953. *Introd. Joseph Campbell. New York: McPherson, Documentext.*

Desmangles, L.G., 2000. *The faces of the gods: Vodou and Roman Catholicism in Haiti.* Univ of North Carolina Press.

Dickens, R. and Torok, A., 2021. *Missing Witches: Recovering True Histories of Feminist Magic.* North Atlantic Books.

Diner, H.R., 1986. *Erin's daughters in America: Irish immigrant women in the nineteenth century.* Johns Hopkins Univ. Press.

Donaldson, Gary A., "A Window on Slave Culture: Dances at Congo Square in New Orleans, 1800–1862." *The Journal of*

Negro History, vol. 69, no. 2, 1984, pp. 63–72. *JSTOR,* https://doi.org/10.2307/2717598. Accessed 5 May 2023.

Dorsey, L., 2020. *Orishas, Goddesses, and Voodoo Queens: The Divine Feminine in the African Religious Traditions.* Weiser Books.

Elliot, J.M. and Angelou, M., 1989. Conversations with Maya Angelou. *(No Title).*

Fandrich, Ina J., "Yorùbá Influences on Haitian Vodou and New Orleans Voodoo." *Journal of Black Studies* 37, no. 5 (2007): 775–91.

Geggus, D., 1991. Haitian Voodoo in the eighteenth century: Language, culture, resistance. *Jahrbuch Für Geschichte Lateinamerikas,* 28(1), pp.21–52.

Giemza, Bryan., "Turned Inside Out: Black, White, and Irish in the South." *Southern Cultures,* vol. 18, no. 1, 2012, pp. 34–57. *JSTOR,* https://www.jstor.org/stable/26217366. Accessed 18 May 2023.

Gilfond, H., 1976. *Voodoo, Its Origins and Practices.* Franklin Watts.

Gimbutas, M., 2001. *The Living Goddesses,* University of California Press.

Gleason, J., 1985. from Oya, in Praise of the Goddess. *Sulfur,* (12), p.62.

Gordon, Michelle Y., "'Midnight Scenes and Orgies': Public Narratives of Voodoo in New Orleans and Nineteenth-Century Discourses of White Supremacy." *American Quarterly,* vol. 64, no. 4, 2012, pp. 767–86. *JSTOR,* http://www.jstor.org/stable/41809523. Accessed 4 May 2023.

Gregory, W. M., "The Cotton Industry." *The Journal of Education,* vol. 74, no. 17 (1852), 1911, pp. 462–63. *JSTOR,* http://www.jstor.org/stable/42819134. Accessed 20 May 2023.

Hilary McD. Beckles., "A 'Riotous and Unruly Lot': Irish Indentured Servants and Freemen in the English West Indies, 1644–1713." *The William and Mary Quarterly* 47, no. 4 (1990): 503–22. https://doi.org/10.2307/2937974. Accesses 17 May 2023.

Hogan, L., McAtackney, L. and Reilly, M.C., 2016. The Irish in the Anglo-Caribbean: servants or slaves? *History Ireland*, 24(2), pp.18–22. Accessed 17 May 2023.Hunt Publishing.

Hurston, Z.N. and Gates, H.L., 2009. *Tell my horse: Voodoo and life in Haiti and Jamaica*. Harper Perennial.

Ina J. Fandrich., "The Birth of New Orleans' Voodoo Queen: A Long-Held Mystery Resolved." *Louisiana History: The Journal of the Louisiana Historical Association*, vol. 46, no. 3, 2005, pp. 293–309. *JSTOR*, http://www.jstor.org/stable/4234122. Accessed 3 May 2023.

Irish in New Orleans - 64 Parishes The influence of Irish immigrants in New Orleans can still be seen in the Irish Channel neighborhood, St. Patrick's Day celebrations and churches such as St. Alphonsus. By Laura D. Kelley.

Jeffers, Honorée Fanonne., "Oya's Rage." *Obsidian III*, vol. 2, no. 1, 2000, pp. 73–74. *JSTOR*.

Kanu, I.A., 2019. African pantheon in a world of change. *Journal of African Studies and Sustainable Development*, 1(3).

Kelley, L.D., 2014. *The Irish in New Orleans*. University of Louisiana at Lafayette Press.

Kelly, E. P., 'Brigid: Pagan Goddess and Christian Saint', *Irish Lives Remembered*, Vol. 53, (2021).

Kelly, E. P., 'Brigid: Pagan Goddess and Christian Saint', *Irish Lives Remembered*, Vol. 53.

Kelly, Liz Childs., 2023. Home to Her at Womancraft Publishing.

Lachance, Paul F., "The 1809 Immigration of Saint-Domingue Refugees to New Orleans: Reception, Integration and Impact." *Louisiana History: The Journal of the Louisiana Historical Association*, vol. 29, no. 2, 1988, pp. 109–41. *JSTOR*, http://www.jstor.org/stable/4232650. Accessed 28 May 2023.

Laguerre, M., 1973. The place of Voodoo in the social structure of Haiti. *Caribbean Quarterly*, 19(3), pp.36–50.

Laguerre, M.S., 2016. *Diasporic citizenship: Haitian Americans in transnational America*. Springer.

Manman Brigitte Rebirth Goddess Order - YouTube.

Marcelin, M., 1949. *Mythologie Vodou (rite arada)* (Vol. 1). Éditions haïtiennes.

Matthewson, Tim., "Jefferson and Haiti." *The Journal of Southern History*, vol. 61, no. 2, 1995, pp. 209–48. *JSTOR*, https://doi.org/10.2307/2211576. Accessed 28 May 2023.

McCaffrey, L., 2004. Ireland and Irish America: Connections and Disconnections. *US Catholic Historian*, 22(3), pp.1–18. Accessed 21 May 2023.

McKinney, Louise., 2006. *Cities of the Imagination* New Orleans, Signal Press.

McLaughlin-Stonham, H., 2020. *From slavery to civil rights: On the streetcars of New Orleans 1830s-present* (p. 272). Liverpool University Press.

McManus, S., 1921. *The story of the Irish race: a popular history of Ireland.* Devin-Adair.

Métraux, A., 2016. *Voodoo in Haiti.* Pickle Partners Publishing.

Murdock, M., 2020. *The Heroine's Journey Workbook: A Map for Every Woman's Quest.* Shambhala Publications.

New Orleans Voodoo." *Western Folklore*, vol. 16, no. 1, 1957, pp. 60–61. *JSTOR*, https://doi.org/10.2307/1497071. Accessed 4 May 2023.

Noonan, K., 2010. Gran Brijit: Haitian Vodou Guardian of the Cemetery. *Goddesses in World Culture*, 3, pp.123–33.

Olupọna, Jacob K., "The Study of Yoruba Religious Tradition in Historical Perspective." *Numen*, vol. 40, no. 3, 1993, pp. 240–73. *JSTOR*, https://doi.org/10.2307/3270151. Accessed 23 July 2023.

Orr, E.R., 2012. *Kissing the Hag: The Dark Goddess and the Unacceptable Nature of Women.* John

Osbey, Brenda Marie., "Why We Can't Talk to You about Voodoo." *The Southern Literary Journal*, vol. 43, no. 2, 2011, pp. 1–11. *JSTOR*, http://www.jstor.org/stable/23208853. Accessed 7 May 2023.

Ray, Benjamin C., "Aladura Christianity: A Yoruba Religion." *Journal of Religion in Africa*, vol. 23, no. 3, 1993, pp. 266–91. *JSTOR*, https://doi.org/10.2307/1581109. Accessed 23 July 2023.

Regan, Joe. "Irish Sugar Planters in Antebellum Louisiana." *History Ireland*, vol. 30, no. 2, 2022, pp. 20–23. *JSTOR*, https://www.jstor.org/stable/27198378. Accessed 20 May 2023.

Rodgers, Nini., "Ireland and the Black Atlantic in the Eighteenth Century." *Irish Historical Studies*, vol. 32, no. 126, 2000, pp. 174–92. *JSTOR*, http://www.jstor.org/stable/30006995. Accessed 25 July 2023.

Saracino, M. and Moser, M. B., She Is Everywhere. *An Anthology of Writings in Womanist/Feminist Spirituality*, Vol. 3, 2012.

Starhawk & Valentine, H., 2011. *The Twelve Wild Swans: A Journey to the Realm of Magic, Healing, and Action*. Harper Collins.

Tann, M.C., 2012., *Haitian Vodou: An Introduction to Haiti's Indigenous Spiritual Tradition*. Llewellyn Worldwide.

Touchstone, Blake., "Voodoo in New Orleans." *Louisiana History: The Journal of the Louisiana Historical Association*, vol. 13, no. 4, 1972, pp. 371–86. *JSTOR*, http://www.jstor.org/stable/4231284. Accessed 1 May 2023.

Weber, C., 2015. *Brigid: History, Mystery, and Magick of the Celtic Goddess*, Weiser Books.

To the Reader

Thank you for purchasing *Maman Brigitte – Dark Goddess of Africa & Ireland*. My sincere hope is that you derived as much from reading this book as I have in creating it. If you have a few moments, please feel free to add your review of the book at your favourite online site for feedback. If you would like to connect with me, please feel free to visit my website paulinebreen.com.

You May Also Like
This is Brigid – Goddess & Saint of Ireland

This is Brigid – Goddess & Saint of Ireland is an informative read on the essence of Brigid in both identities as Goddess and Saint. From a historical perspective we can see how Celtic Irish society venerated the divine feminine as well as other gods and goddesses. Out of this society emerged Brigid, Ireland's most cherished female deity who is still considered today to be the triple goddess of Poetry, Healing and Smithcraft amongst others. Information is presented on Brigid as daughter of the Dagda, partner of Bres and mother to Ruadan. Her eternal presence is explored in the four elements of Fire, Water, Earth and Air, in the natural landscape all around us and in the various stages of womanhood witnessed in Maiden, Lover, Mother, Queen and Crone.

As Catholic Saint her early life and her many miraculous feats contain similar undertones to that of the Goddess. In her lore as Saint, we see examples of a strong, independent woman who knew her own mind and followed her own heart and life path.

Who is Brigid? Goddess or Saint or both? In what expression of her do you find connection? How does she relate to a modern audience? Learn about Brigid in her two distinctive but overlapping considerations and find ways to see her aliveness and ever presence in today's world.

ISBN: 9798365684454

MOON BOOKS
PAGANISM & SHAMANISM

What is Paganism? A religion, a spirituality, an alternative belief system, nature worship? You can find support for all these definitions (and many more) in dictionaries, encyclopedias, and text books of religion, but subscribe to any one and the truth will evade you. Above all Paganism is a creative pursuit, an encounter with reality, an exploration of meaning and an expression of the soul. Druids, Heathens, Wiccans and others, all contribute their insights and literary riches to the Pagan tradition. Moon Books invites you to begin or to deepen your own encounter, right here, right now.

If you have enjoyed this book, why not tell other readers by posting a review on your preferred book site.

Readers of ebooks can buy or view any of these bestsellers by clicking on the live link in the title. Most titles are published in paperback and as an ebook. Paperbacks are available in traditional bookshops. Both print and ebook formats are available online.

Find more titles and sign up to our readers' newsletter
www.collectiveinkbooks.com/paganism

For video content, author interviews and more, please subscribe to our YouTube channel.

MoonBooksPublishing

Follow us on social media for book news, promotions and more:

Facebook: Moon Books

Instagram: @MoonBooksCI

X: @MoonBooksCI

TikTok: @MoonBooksCI